ALLIED DUNBAR LIBRARY

MONEY GUIDES

YOUR HOME IN ITALY

ALLIED DUNBAR LIBRARY

MONEY GUIDES

YOUR HOME IN ITALY

FLAVIA MAXWELL

LONGMAN

ISBN 0-85121-521-1

Published by

Longman Law, Tax and Finance
Longman Group UK Limited
21-27 Lamb's Conduit Street, London WC1N 3NJ

Associated Offices

Australia, Hong Kong, Malaysia, Singapore, USA

A CIP catalogue record for this book is available from the British Library.

Printed in Great Britain by Biddles of Guildford Ltd., Surrey

Foreword

As someone who has a long connection with Italy I am grateful to Allied Dunbar to have the opportunity to give readers of this book some idea of the joys and pitfalls of building or owning property in this delightful country. There is a lot more to benefiting from property ownership in Italy, whether you live there full time or on a holiday basis only, than simply avoiding legal pitfalls. You must get to know the Italians which should not be a difficult task as they are always intensely interested in anyone new to the district. They will tolerate your dreadful Italian but you must make the effort to have at least a smattering of their language, which is simple in the early stages and only gets difficult later on with the advent of complicated tenses. You will quickly learn to enjoy all that is best in Italy.

'Living in Italy' by Yve Menzies which is published by Robert Hale will in this respect provide an admirable companion to this book. Not only does it cover subjects of which you will need to know more if you are to buy in Italy, and which are outside the scope of this book, but it also gives an insight into why the Italians are as they are and will help you to get the maximum pleasure out of your home in Italy. The quotations from the book which appear in the text are with the permission of its author and her publishers.

Finally, probably more than any other country in Europe, Italy's most important asset is her people and although without them there would be a great deal to see and appreciate most British, once settled here, enthuse about the Italians and their attitude to life in general.

Contents

1 Introduction

Buying property in Italy presents problems and opportunities for British purchasers that are quite different from those found in countries such as Spain. In Italy property development has not taken place solely with a foreign market in mind, although foreigners' money is of course just as welcome. Occasionally you find places which seem to 'belong' to Germans or Dutch but this is relatively rare. One of the main advantages of having a house or flat in Italy is that you reap the full benefit of being abroad. You will not lead an isolated existence shut off in an exclusively British development surrounded by shops and services which depend on foreign custom for their existence. The Italians are far too gregarious to allow national ghettos to be built, and anyway, in the nicest possible way, they want to know what is going on. Life in Italy and the way of doing things is often even more different than the proverbial chalk from cheese.

Some history

Italy is steeped in history, much of it admittedly bloodthirsty but much of it also of infinite worth to the world at large. For those who wish to take advantage of it, it can be like living in an artistic paradise. Some of the Tuscan towns and cities possess inestimable art treasures on show for all to see, often, in the case of statues and churches, in the street. The locals take this treasure house very calmly, seemingly too calmly at times when little is done to protect them and even less is done about restoring them or keeping them in good condition. At least most of the churches have learnt to keep their doors locked when there is no one present, in order to safeguard the silver and artifacts but it is still a national scandal that so much is stolen from both churches and country museums.

Few people can afford to invest in a large 16th century Tuscan villa or a Venetian palazzo but there are plenty of houses and farms to be had all over Italy which are more than four or five hundred years old. Moreover, the Italian builders in the area are nearly always very talented and artistic when it comes to restoring and bringing them up to date. Modern Italian architecture — even blocks of flats — often leaves something to be desired. It frequently has a monolithic quality although, again, there are well designed and landscaped blocks of flats to be had.

Reasons for buying in Italy

No-one should contemplate buying property in Italy without knowing exactly why he wants to do so and, therefore, what it is that he should look to buy. This may sound obvious but although the average Englishman has some idea of what goes on in the property market in England, he is unlikely to have any 'feel' about Italy. What he must remember is that although he may buy in an area popular with foreigners, there is no reason to suppose that he will be buying from or ultimately selling to a foreigner. The Italian from Milan or Turin seeks the sun just as much as the Swede from Goteborg or the German from Cologne. The house market is therefore not a 'tourist' market and the English buyer or seller takes his chance with the rest. There is no shortage of estate agents in Italy; if anything, there are too many. This is because they tend to be very local in the range of property they have on their books. Buying through agencies or at exhibitions in the UK is sometimes used for special developments by British companies in Sardinia, Tuscany or

Umbria etc, but it is not necessarily the best way to buy. You really should go out and look around for yourself since such developments are usually more highly priced than what is available locally and will, therefore, be more difficult to sell later on.

Apart from saying that there should be absolutely no question of buying solely with a view to a quick capital profit, it is extremely difficult to say whether any particular 'buy' will in the end turn out to be a good investment. On the whole, prices have, in the last ten years at least, kept pace with inflation but not necessarily with the fall in the value of the lira, although obviously the odd quick profits have been made. Building costs are going up all the time as are labour costs. It pays to do what the Italians do, buy a house and stay put if possible. Changing houses can be expensive and it is worthwhile making the right choice first time round, depending on your probable future plans — a holiday home that will always remain a family holiday home or something which can later become a retirement home or perhaps just land to build on one day (although this option can have problems if you are in an area where building permission only lasts for three years). Remember also, that from time to time, density regulations change and you may well be able to build in the future something that was impossible to contemplate when you first bought your property. Density regulations in Italy seldom reduce the volume allowed per square metre which is a comforting thought.

What this book is all about

The intention of this book is to explain how property — house, flat or land — is bought in Italy. What you must remember (without in the least being discouraged) is that you are buying a home in a foreign country and so:

- The contract you will be asked to sign will be not only in

Italian but in legal Italian and it may be one of a number of different types of contract; all other documents involved will be in similar Italian.
- The Italian legal system is wholly different from the English legal system.
- The Italian tax system is different from the English tax system.

There is no reason to expect that you know any of the rules but there is every reason to hope that you will take expert advice about those rules for which, of course, you must be prepared to pay. You would not try to buy a house in England without the services of a solicitor. To attempt to do so abroad without similar assistance is not only foolhardy but, in the case of purchases in Italy, can, as you will read later on, end up as an expensive mistake.

Be prepared to get advice

You have taken the first step; you have bought this book. The question is where do you go now for the kind of advice you will need to make certain that the pitfalls you now know exist are avoided? What must you do to make certain that your purchase is not only properly dealt with from an Italian legal point of view but also takes account, if it is a holiday home, that you are still living in England or if it is a retirement home, of your British nationality and background. Ideally, the person to advise you is someone with a considerable knowledge of, and practical experience in both English and Italian law who preferably lives in Italy, though this is not essential. It may be that your own solicitor has such a contact but one of the best alternative sources of information is the local British Consul. Although he is not officially allowed to recommend anyone, he is unlikely to send you to someone he knows to be unreliable. This is of considerable importance because in all probability you will be advised to give that person a Power of Attorney to act for you on completion and generally to look after your interests. Usually that person can also give British references which you can take up.

A word of warning

Italian consumer protection law covers a wide variety of situations, much of it relating to property purchases and building goes back a number of years. In theory, there is likely to be a rule or regulation available to deal with most of what could go wrong in most cases. The difficulty is that theory is not practice. If you have a building problem it is likely to be either because your builder has failed to complete the building on time or has not fulfilled the specifications. Not much can help you if your builder has 'gone bust', (although even then something can be done if you are prepared to wait a very long time).

The law can help you if building is not progressing according to your contract but the Italian legal system is incredibly slow. Often it will take at least two years to get to court and about 50% of all cases in Italy go to appeal (another two years). It goes without saying that your building contract should have stringent penalty clauses. To inflict these penalty clauses you must consult a lawyer (who should have drawn up the contract anyway with the help of the architect or *geometrà*) and he will go to the local *Tribunale* and arrange this. However, like all good lawyers he will try and settle the matter first. It is to be hoped that you will not get to this stage.

If you have problems with the country house you have purchased because your neighbour insists that he has a right of way over your garden, something of which you knew nothing about, or you find that half a dozen surrounding owners are helping themselves to your water supply, the lawyers will be delighted to solve your problem but it may take years to do so. However, it should be remembered that easements and access to a water supply by other people **must** be shown on your conveyance — without such evidence your neighbours do not stand a chance. The moral is, if you can't avoid every problem, at least avoid as many as you can by taking the right advice from the right person from the very beginning.

As always, it is correct information at the right time which provides the answer to a problem and the right time is before the problem arises. This book is intended to help in this direction by taking a look at the matters you should bear in mind when you are about to become involved in property transactions in Italy. It is written in general terms and so is not meant to take the place of specific advice about a particular situation. Do not treat it as a DIY guide to buying and selling Italian property but it is hoped that it will be of general interest and will help you to avoid the pitfalls and to understand the advice and help which you should seek.

2 Where to buy

The climate

This must surely be the main reason for most Northern Europeans coming to Italy but even on this score you should stop and think for a minute. 'Sunny' Italy has many climates although one can more or less guarantee an abundance of sunshine everywhere in the summer months. Of course, in the Alpine regions in the north of the country one must expect heavy snow for months at a time but if one is a skier then this is obviously ideal. However other parts of Italy are also mountainous — the Appenines for instance and you should consider the autumn and winter climate a moment before you rush off and buy in hilly Umbria. Piedmont and Lombardy can be as cold as Copenhagen in winter though the wind is never as bad.

Then there is the question of rain. There is never enough in Italy but there are places that get too much for a holiday maker at certain times of the year. Therefore, if you are really affronted by rainy days on holiday you should head for the more arid regions of the South such as Calabria, Apulia and Sicily, though even there you will get the odd thunderstorm. Of course, without rain you cannot garden, except in the Mexican fashion with cacti and succulents, so keen gardeners who are buying to live in Italy as opposed to merely taking holidays, should take even more notice of the climate.

Never listen to locals about the weather. In every country in the world they seem to lie about it. Unless it is sunny, it is, as a well-known film location researcher has always found,

Source: The Italian State Tourist Office.

'most unusual sort of weather for this time of year' though when you look up the records you get a totally different story. Many resorts, particularly those on the Italian Riviera and the Tuscan coast boast about their micro-climates, though I can say from personal experience that Bordighera and Sanremo seem to enjoy a micro-climate and are always considerably warmer than our town only a few kilometres away.

The great thing to look for in micro-climates is **lack** of huge differences between summer and winter temperatures and Sanremo boasts of a mere ten degrees centigrade difference over the whole year. What is growing in the public parks and the street trees which are planted are also an indication. The presence of well-grown false-pepper trees (*Schinus molle*) or Jacaranda means that it **cannot** get very cold in winter. Hotel gardens and parks bedded out with cyclamen in winter are a good sign to the sun lover. Bougainvillea all over the houses means there is very little or no frost. However, masses of bedding plants and pleached limes can often mean hot summers and cold winters.

Tourism

Two other things are important in Italy — possibly more so than in Britain. First, it is a very long country — the longest in Europe, and although round the north and the industrial part of Lombardy and Piedmont communications by motorway are excellent this is not so all over the country. Therefore, it can take you a long time to get to, or escape from, your chosen area. Secondly, because of its unique historical buildings and art treasures, to say nothing of its climate, Italy is tourist orientated. This is wonderful if you come as a tourist but if you live in a tourist centre you can end up wondering whether living in Florence, Sienna, Venice or Rome is all that you are led to expect it to be. True, tourists tend to push up the prices but at the same time they do improve the amenities available, not least restaurants. You must choose where to live very carefully and consider whether you will mind your home town full of foreigners (you won't be one for long) for five or six months of the year. If you do, then do not choose one of the large tourist centres or coastal resorts since they can be too busy in the season and absolutely dead in winter, though of course large cities have a life of their own anyway — tourism notwithstanding.

Where to buy

The British have been buying in Italy for literally hundreds of years — indeed for longer than in any other country in Europe except possibly around Bordeaux in France. They have always had their favourite parts but these are presently changing. There used to be a large British colony in Sicily which hardly exists today and much of the Riviera dei Fiori between Ventimiglia and Alassio was very British — Sanremo was the chic place to have a villa — and it still is. Tuscany was and still is a great British stamping ground but, alas, except in the deepest country, has become far too expensive for the second home market. And then of course there are the lakes, Como, Garda, Maggiore, etc, where the British built magnificent villas and gardens for the summer season (since in winter it is foggy and damp there). Most of the British have sold now, tempted by unheard of riches from Milanese millionaires.

Tuscany

Region by region, Tuscany in Central Italy is still the most popular with the British and people will pay over the top for something they could get for two thirds of the price in neighbouring Umbria and half the price in the Marches on the Adriatic — the latter on the coast moreover. Why? Because the British like to find other British around them and there are plenty of them in Tuscany. Apart from the cities, Tuscany is the most expensive country region, except the lakes, in Italy with London estate agents advertising Tuscan farms from £80,000 upwards! Houses are cheaper on the spot and there are still bargains to be had around Arezzo and north of Lucca.

Off the beaten track, however, communications are not brilliant and the Tuscan coastal resorts which are crowded in summer and lonely, foggy and windswept in winter are not recommended for year round living. Anything within 30 kilometres of Florence, Sienna, Pisa or the main tourist cities will be considerably more expensive. Water and electricity can be a problem in deep Tuscan countryside but getting building help (and good workmen at that) is easy. Therefore, you should check, or have checked by your own *geometrà*, such things before signing any form of contract. Remember, it is easy to make your own electricity but lack of water can be a big problem. Farms usually have a source of water but ordinary country houses often relied on rainfall, which is not recommended in the 20th century!

Umbria

Next to Tuscany lies Umbria which is becoming very popular and so prices are rising all the time. Lago Trasimeno is very sought after but full time residents (as opposed to summer visitors) should bear in mind that the area is well known for being foggy. Prices are very much lower, however, than in Tuscany and unlike that region you will not find so many British there. Perugia is a beautiful place to visit but with the tourists in summer and the international university students for the rest of the year not everyone would want to live there all year round.

The Marches

The Marches, which have an Adriatic coastline, are a lovely

part of Italy and much under-rated. Somewhat difficult to get to but served by two airports, they are divided into four provinces, Pescara, Ancona, Macerata and Ascoli Piceno and all are endowed with beautiful architecture. Granted, there has been some undesirable coastal development but away from the resorts and towns there are still lovely, sandy beaches to laze on and plenty of not too high mountains to walk in. Except inland and upland the winters are not severe and on the coast you can rely on being frost free all year round.

Emilia-Romagna

Emilia-Romagna is a vast province and acts as no-man's land between the industrial north and the agricultural centre and south of the country. Except for a tiny piece of Liguria it straddles Italy from East to West. It is mostly flat, watered by the Po and its tributaries, and is where a great deal of Italy's farming produce comes from, including Parmesan cheese which comes from Parma of course, but also from Ferrara and Modena. Having been a Papal State until the Unification of Italy it has a wonderful architectural heritage. Bologna is the provincial capital as well as being the gastronomic capital of Italy. The food is rich and heavy but the local wines are not wonderful and you would be wise to order your wines from Tuscany or Piedmont instead. In spite of having towns such as history-steeped Ferrara and Ravenna not many foreigners choose to live in Emilia-Romagna. Except in the large cities it is not particularly expensive to buy property there. However, such farms as there are for sale are large and not many small country houses are on the market.

Venetia

Altogether different are the three north eastern regions of Venetia, Alto-Adige and the autonomous region of Friuli-Venezia-Giulia. Venetia has everything to offer the foreigner from mountains to sea, architecture and history and the most beautiful stately homes in the world, and of course, it has Venice (not that anyone would advise **living** in Venice). It is far better to live in the Veneto (Venetia) and visit Venice from time to time. Nowhere in Italy, not even Rome or Milan is as expensive as Venice, yet, as the Italians say, '*Ci sono posti,*' meaning if you know your way about you don't need to pay the earth for an hotel (the Daniele or the Gritti can be £600 a night), a meal or a handbag. Both Asolo and around Conegliano are popular with the British and foreigners generally and are only 45 minutes from Venice or her airport. But Venetia contains other beautiful towns such as Padua, Verona, Vicenza all of which have a delightful hinterland in which you will find famous Palladio villas and beautiful churches.

Right in the north of the region is the province of Belluno, high in the mountains. There are many ski resorts here, including Cortina d'Ampezzo and you must pay for the privilege of living in such a resort. Elsewhere however, it is much, much cheaper. Overall, Venetia is not expensive and there are old farms, small vineyards, (Venetia contributes generously to the EC wine lake) and village houses to be had at reasonable prices. There is no problem about water here but if you are high up a mountain you may have to generate your own electricity (which is not difficult).

The weather in this region is very reliable (this is the kindest thing to be said about it). Long, hot summers go on until the end of October but spring is late arriving and short. The winters are long too with plenty of rain and fog and of course, if you are in the mountains, plenty of snow. Therefore, it is an ideal place for a summer holiday home.

Alto-Adige

Much the same can be said about the two other regions although they are less sophisticated than Venetia itself. Alto-Adige which includes the tourists' paradise Trentino is very

Austrian orientated, the food is solid and copious and the wine is excellent. Much of the population speaks German and they generally regard foreigners as passing, not staying, so on a permanent basis you may not feel so comfortable. Overall it is not very Italian, it was, after all, part of the Austro-Hungarian Empire until 1918.

Friuli-Venezia-Giulia

A considerable part of Friuli-Venezia-Giulia used to be owned by the Austro-Hungarians too. Here, the foreign influence is Slav or more accurately, Slovene. The people are said to be the most honest in Italy and the most hard-working. The cost of housing is less than Venetia but there is not so much available so you will have to build.

Udine is a province which is ideal for summer holidays, full of beautiful architecture and reminders of Venice's presence everywhere. Prices have gone up since it was linked up to the Milan–Venice motorway but they are still relatively reasonable. The city itself has the most dramatic backdrop in Europe of the Carnic Alps.

The weather throughout the region, except in summer when it is hot in the day and cool at night, is rather cool and can be damp. But the scenery is magnificent. Rolling hills covered in vines, dramatic snow-covered mountains and many examples of Venetian architecture abound. Strangely, the short sea coast of this province is not particularly sought after since it has too many rivers debouching into it. This lagoon type of coastline is fine for birdwatching but not much else although there are Italians who swear by Grado as a resort.

Almost on its own lies the tiny province and large city of Trieste which for 800 years was Austria-Hungary's main port and has only been Italian for less than a tenth of that time. You will hear as much Slovene and Hungarian in the city as you will Italian. The place is well organised ('it's still an

Austrian town'; Italians frequently joke) and the people are charming and very good looking.

Behind Trieste lies the Carso, a barren area of limestone rock with very dramatic scenery. The weather for half the year is terrible but the summers are long, hot and dry — though very subject to squalls and thunderstorms. All in all, Trieste and its province seem to be places to visit rather than live. Friuli-Venezia-Giulia is not expensive for property and the houses are extremely well built but you must think of large heating costs if you are going to live there all the year round. The locals, rather like the Spaniards, sit round a sort of half open stove called a *fogher* which will warm those nearest to it but not much else.

Lombardy

Lombardy is the richest region of Italy with Milan as its capital. Just north of Milan is a region of lakes and property which near, or particularly on these lakes is extremely expensive, possibly **the** most expensive in Italy. Dismiss any idea of a lakeside house on Como — it is for multi-millionaires. Lombardy includes much of Italy's industry around Milan, Parma and Pavia so those places do not seem particularly suitable unless you are attracted by the industry. Bergamo in the mountains is almost as expensive as the lakes.

The main problem with Lombardy is that the locals have bought up most of the desirable property a long time ago. Quite apart from the astronomical prices in the resorts, Lombardy is the most expensive region in Italy in which to buy property. Moreover the climate is problematic, hence the desirability of the mountains and the lakes, consisting of stifling summers, foggy autumns, bitter winters and wet springs.

Piedmont

Less expensive and infinitely more desirable than Lombardy is the region of Piedmont. The wine and food are good, the scenery beautiful and the prices are moderate except for Turin and its environs. If you want the sea you are out of luck but the region's province of Novara shares Lake Maggiore with Lombardy and has its own lake called Lago di Orta which must be one of the most beautiful lakes in the world (complete with a town in the middle of it). Of course, prices round the lakes are high but there are places nearby and inland which can be bought relatively cheaply. The further from Turin airport the cheaper the property, but do not forget that Milan has another airport apart from Linate called Malpensa which serves the Piedmont provinces of Varese, Alessandria and in particular Novara. It is also the cheaper airport to fly to (the 'Gatwick' of Milan) and is very useful.

One area popular with the British (and the Dutch and Germans) is around the hills of Asti (of Spumante fame) and Alba (of truffle fame). The Langhe hills are beautiful and full of excellent wine, restaurants and pleasant, hard-working people. The summers are hot or warm depending how high up the mountain you are but the winters are wet and cold. It proves an ideal spot for a summer holiday home and is not expensive.

Aosta

The Aosta region is often considered part and parcel of Piedmont although strictly speaking it is not. It is situated in the Italian Alps and contains the Italian part of Mont Blanc. Some British like it because they don't have to learn Italian but can speak French there, since it is an official language in this region. Property for foreigners is confined mostly to ski-resorts such as Courmayeur and prices are higher than in Piedmont's ski resorts. It is distinctly cool in summer but snow in winter is guaranteed. Chalets and apartments are extremely well built and combine the best of Italian and French design and workmanship. The people are not very gregarious and tend to keep to themselves.

Liguria

The one remaining region in the north and the smallest in Italy, is Liguria, once a British stronghold but it now seems to have been deserted a little for the French Côte d'Azur of which it is a continuation. Now that no one is allowed to build within 300 metres of the sea such properties in Liguria command an enormous price, as do flats in resorts such as Bordighera, Ospedaletti, Sanremo, Alassio, Santa Margherita, Portofino, etc. There are a fair amount of properties to be had in the hinterland which rises quickly to 2000 feet and is therefore cold in winter. Those that command a sea-view also command a higher price even though the sea view often includes a view of the motorway and a great number of carnation greenhouses, as anyone who has seen the scenery around Sanremo can vouch. Greenhouses are the scourge of Ligurian scenery and it is difficult to find a good view, due south, without them in it since these are just what is needed to grow the carnations, hothouse roses, freesias, orchids etc that come from this area.

The western end of the Italian Riviera is served by Nice Airport in France but the other side is best served from Genoa. There is land available for building but good builders are booked up and are mostly very expensive. There is not much help around as the area is full of people 'doing their own thing' ie growing flowers for the North European market, the UK included. The food, particularly the fish, is excellent and expensive and the wine poor and expensive in restaurants (far better to choose something from neighbouring Piedmont). The area is packed with non-Italians, with the French heading the list followed by the Germans, Dutch and British.

Sicily

Sicily used to be popular with the British, especially in and around Taormina in the province of Messina but this island is busy making itself a very ugly, urban jungle. The climate is hot and dry all year round, too hot in summer for most people and there is a permanent water shortage. Unless you have a great interest in Greek remains and archaeology then Sicily has probably lost its appeal for most Northern Europeans quite apart from the fact that it is so far away that only a fly-drive holiday is possible.

Sardinia

The situation is a little better on the Costa Smeralda in Sardinia but here again the winters are cold and wet and it is not really a place for year round occupation unless you have really got yourself set up. Prices on the Costa Smeralda are astronomical and attract a certain type of person — the multi-millionaires. Nature is truly 'in the raw' in the rest of Sardinia and although you may be able to buy an Hermes scarf or a pair of Gucci shoes in the season on the Costa Smeralda you will find it difficult to buy a steak or an avocado pear anywhere on the island for the rest of the year. Not without reason, Mussolini used Sardinia as a place of *confino* for anti-Fascists whom he wanted to be kind to (other places were much more terrible) and even today government workers, non-Sardinians that is, regard working in Sardinia as a hardship post.

The South

The regions of Abruzzo, Apulia (Puglia), Basilicata, Molise and Calabria all have limited appeal for the holiday maker though they are packed with history, marvellous architecture and archaeological sites, particularly Calabria and Puglia. They are the poorest regions of Italy and there are whole villages which are empty because their occupants have gone to live and work elsewhere. Except at altitude, all these regions are arid and the sun shines virtually all year. In the mountains life is even harder.

Latina (Latium)

Left until last are the regions of Campania of which the regional capital is Naples and Latina (also known as Latium or Lazio) of which the regional capital is also the national, Rome. Rome and its neighbouring hills are expensive areas to live and, as in Milan, the locals have bought all the best places at the best prices long ago. Occasionally there are properties to be had at reasonable prices in attractive locations — and near Rome — but such joy is relatively rare. It is a long process trying to find the right property at the right price in this part of Italy and wanting something by the sea makes it doubly so. In the other provinces of Viterbo, Rieti and Frosinone prices are much more reasonable, as they are in the province of Latina but you will realise that once away from Rome, Latina is already a southern region where things do not move fast.

Campania

Campania contains, apart from Naples, three resorts much beloved of the British, Amalfi, Sorrento and Capri — all of them ruinously expensive for the property buyer. It also contains the poorest province in the whole of Italy, Avellino. Looking at the city this is not immediately apparent and must have something to do with the unemployment rate and/ or tax returns or both. Prices are reasonable and there are plenty of people, who are well qualified, looking for work whose family obligations do not allow them the usual southern choice of emigration to the north. Summers are very long and very hot and water proves a big problem. Spring and autumn are the best seasons — winters are mild and damp.

Sample the region first

Once you have decided on an area you think you will like it is probably best to rent an apartment or house there before you finally decide to pay out for something you may not like or which may be difficult to sell later on. If you are buying for full-time use it is as well to know your choice of area all the year round. Winter can be a rude (and expensive) experience in what you believed to be 'sunny' Italy.

Travelling to Italy is not a problem. It has international airports and many local airports. It also has a good motorway system in the north and down to Florence and Rome but even with the Channel tunnel the car journey from the UK is still a long one to more or less any part of Italy. Much of the motorway system is free in the south while in the north you pay hefty motorway tolls, particularly in Liguria and parts of Tuscany. Car hire, whilst not cheap, is less expensive than in many parts of Europe — remember you will not be able to hire a car (in theory) without an international driving licence since the Italians like to see a photograph. They also like you to use credit cards rather than cash.

3 What to buy

There is virtually every type of property on sale in every architectural style. Most of it has been built for years. There is occasionally the possibility of buying an apartment in a block which has not yet been built. This has special advantages and even more special difficulties of which more elsewhere in this book.

Summer residence

If you are not going to live in Italy permanently but only for summer holidays then it is less important that your house is situated in an area which is known to be cold in winter. Provided it is well built and well insulated and watertight you need consider little else. Do not however buy a house with even a medium sized garden since gardeners are not easy to come by in Italy and they are often unreliable as to when they will turn up — particularly if they know you are not on hand to chivvy them. You can well return to a house surrounded by burnt grass, weeds and the occasional dead flower. For that sort of purchase a flat in a resort or in a block with a swimming pool (make sure it is big enough for all the summer residents to use without being crowded) is a better bet. Moreover, for some reason, your neighbour will be more reliable about watering your balcony than will a gardener.

Long-term residence

If, however, you are considering long-term or permanent residence then a house is probably a better answer particularly when you take into account how much you have to pay for a flat to get total privacy, peace and quiet. This is frankly a question of class. At one end of the scale come the remote and stand-offish but also quiet people. At the other end of the scale come the noisy, inquisitive, friendly and helpful. You must choose what sort of neighbours you want and pay accordingly.

Rural areas

It would be stupid to take a village house if you were a quiet, shy and contemplative creature. You will get little peace from morning till night and they probably will not even be talking to you but only to each other. In any event it is noisy, full of life and local colour. Houses and conversions to houses come in all shapes and sizes, from a farmer's cottage to an apartment in a castle.

Certain parts of Italy are, out of the towns, very peasant orientated and there are few farms, large houses and castles. Central Italy abounds in castles, vineyards, *fattorie* or *tenute* (both farms or small-holdings), *poderi* which are another type of small-holding or estate but one which still functions as a going concern. There are *poderi* which have wine or olives as their main crop but others which were part of a share-cropping system now more or less disappeared in Italy. One of the reasons that Tuscany became so popular was that there was always something for sale since so many farmers and land workers were emigrating to the north of Italy or to the UK or the USA. Now that source has dried up one must look farther afield in Umbria, the Marches or parts of Emilia-Romagna.

New buildings and conversions

Such new building as goes on in Italy is largely concerned with conversion of old properties. There are problems with this. Very often they have to be sold since getting a building licence will depend on being able to build two floors, each having ceilings 2.75 metres high. If the house has three floors this is easily possible but not if it only has two. Only village houses are exempt from this ceiling height in order to keep the buildings in accord with each other. Out in the country the purchase of an old farm house may involve you in raising the roof, the ceiling of the ground floor and the installation of very complicated and expensive drainage.

The Italians as yet are not great converters of barns and anyway except in the northern regions there are not many that are not still being used. Very occasionally you will see an advertisement for a *granaio* for sale, with planning permission for conversion to a dwelling house — but it is a rare occurrence. Stables and coach houses come into the same category except that usually they have already been converted for the rest of the family to come home to in the summer holidays. Some of these conversions particularly in north-eastern Italy can be very well done if you are lucky enough to find one.

The problem with houses or blocks of flats in seaside resorts is that they are often built in a rather flimsy fashion for summer occupancy only. The Tuscan coast is littered with such buildings and the place is dead out of season. This is one of the few parts of Italy which can look suburban in the worst sense of the term. However, if the resort is a fairly large town in its own right such as Amalfi, Sanremo or the seaside which serves Rome you will be able to find every sort and every quality of building.

Because of the weather and the frequent hard winters the northern regions of Italy build more solidly than do those of the south where the main consideration is how to keep cool.

Central Italy strikes a balance between the two and apart from the provinces of Verona, Vicenza and Venetia (Veneto) it probably has the most beautiful buildings in Italy.

To build new property on land with planning permission takes courage, money and a great deal of patience. What you gain financially you lose in patience. Apart from the rule that you must keep more or less to the local style you will get what you want, where you want and one hopes it will be trouble free for many years to come. This is not always the case with old property in Italy; scarcely surprising since some of the farms and village houses are between 300 and 500 years old.

4 What to do and what not to do

This chapter is in the nature of a quick run-down on the main things you should bear in mind when you are buying property in Italy. The basic problem is that most British buyers of property in Italy are used to the British system where, for all the complaints that have been made over the past few years about the legal profession, buyers have been cossetted by their solicitors who have guided them through the trauma of house purchase. There is no equivalent of this service in Italy. The system expects you, in the majority of cases, to sign a contract prepared by an estate agent virtually without any previous enquiries and without the services of a surveyor. You are expected to make your own mortgage arrangements. You are expected to sign a complicated purchase document in front of a notary who (quite properly) is also acting for the seller and is almost certainly without any explanations which you can readily understand. Finally, you will normally have to deal with the insurance of the property when you have bought it, whereas you are used to your solicitor doing this automatically for you over the phone within minutes of completing the purchase.

Do not be in any way put off by all this. The solution is to apply your ordinary British outlook to your purchase in Italy and entrust it to a suitable adviser (preferably in Italy) who will look after your interests as far as possible as though you were buying in England.

Think of what you would do if you were buying property in the UK. You would:

- Not necessarily buy the first house or flat you saw.
- Not sign a contract presented to you by the seller's agent but arrange for it to be sent to your solicitor.
- Work out carefully your financial situation and consult your bank manager or accountant or solicitor, not only to see if you could afford the price asked but how you could best raise it.
- If you were buying with a mortgage loan, get the offer of that loan before exchanging contracts or make the contract conditional on that offer.
- If what you were buying was a 'second home', get your tax position clarified.

When you had decided that the house was what you were looking for and that you could afford it, you would go ahead in the knowledge that your solicitor would protect you from all the legal problems.

The Italian system

The same sort of rules apply to buying property in Italy but they are dealt with in an Italian way. The Italians cannot normally get all that advice out of one person and have to do some of the work themselves or employ their lawyer or accountant to do it for them. It should be borne in mind that Italian notaries are forbidden by law to arrange mortgages or even recommend mortgage institutions beyond suggesting that you go to a bank or company which specialises in house mortgages. The solution is to treat yourself to the same sort of protection as you would in Britain. Added to this, there is the obvious problem that even if you speak Italian reasonably well, you do not speak legal and technical Italian. There are differences in outlook between the Italians and the British and certain tax problems can arise. You may find it difficult to negotiate and get the kind of information you need to help you make up your mind.

Building contracts

Truly fraudulent builders are rare, bankrupt builders are more common — you need not fear that you will be 'fiddled' any more than if you were Italian but the Italians get 'fiddled' too. Do not sign building contracts put in front of you by builders without advice (would you do so in England?) and do not use architects recommended to you by builders. Even the other way round can be dangerous. Let your chosen expert in Italy check out both architect and builder. Moreover, no building contract should be entered into which does not contain fearsome penalty clauses. If you do not have these, the builders will be busy attending to those contracts which do contain such clauses and then who knows when your house will be finished. Finally, never commence **any** building work, no matter how small, without permission from the local town hall. You or your attorney will have to sign for this permission, known as a *licenza* at the local town hall or *municipio* and you should start nothing, not even the foundations without this piece of paper in your hands. Take no notice of any builder or architect who tells you otherwise — you will pay the fine not him.

Watch your budget

Never over commit yourself. Wild fluctuations in the sterling/lira rate are unlikely but the minimum time between finding your property and completing will probably not be less than six weeks. Also the general consensus of opinion is that you tend to get a more generous sterling/lira rate from banks in England than from banks in Italy. Even a 25 lire difference can mount up when you are spending at least 50 million lire on a house; in fact a 1.25 million lire difference.

From the time you decide you want to buy, and think that you have enough available cash, to the date of completion will be a much longer period than in England. If you are buying a flat or house which has not yet been completed, you will probably have to spread stage payments over at least six months to a year. It is not so much a currency crisis against the lira that you have to worry about but spiralling costs. The inflation rate in Italy is currently not great but inflation exists and if you are building a house over a relatively long period you will need protective conditions in your contract.

The legal side

Do engage the services of the right kind of adviser in Italy. In Tuscany, Rome, Milan and to a lesser degree round Venice there are English lawyers with a knowledge of Italian law who can help you. Next on the list come Italian lawyers and accountants (*commercialisti*) who speak English and last of all, for those who speak Italian, the same Italian lawyers and accountants but without English. Do not dismiss them merely because their English is not good or non-existent. It is one of these people who will draw up your conditions in the *compromesso* (the contract) and who will be protecting **your** interests.

Sign nothing without consulting the adviser you have chosen to look after your interests and never pay money over without his advice. If you feel that you must make some payment without being covered in this way, only make payments in favour of a notary, never the estate agent. For building land you can stipulate you will pay nothing and sign nothing unless you have the written up to date *licenza*. Italian building permission can lapse after one year or after three years and you must watch the date. Also this is the moment to find out whether the *licenza* has been paid for. Normally, it is the responsibility of the purchaser and not of the vendor.

If you are offered documents which have been translated into English for you to consider at your leisure, be extremely wary of what they say. Many will be written in inadequate English: the most dangerous are those which are written in reasonably good English but put Italian legal terms into what the translator thought were the equivalent English legal terms. Some results are amusing — most are terribly misleading. It is not fair to take such papers home to show your solicitor and expect him to tell you if they are in order, unless he has some knowledge of Italian law.

Tax implications

A word on tax. You need not worry that all taxes due on the completion of a purchase in Italy will not be paid. The notary will never complete until he has in hand all the cash necessary to enable him to make these payments. Annual taxes in respect of Italian property are normally payable in arrears at the end of the year. You usually have about two months in which to pay, after which between two and 20% is added to the bill — payment even later than this can mean a heavy fine. Unless the annual taxes and INVIM have been paid by the vendor the transfer document cannot be prepared, so you can be assured you will not be paying any of the vendor's unpaid tax.

The Italian Government charges 17% stamp duty on land transfers and this high figure is based on the assumption that approximately one-third only of the price will be disclosed in the documents. It is not advised that you should adhere to this plan since it can land you with an enormous capital gains tax bill (INVIM) because you are artificially reducing the purchase price to say nothing of getting a proper mortgage which is based on the price in the transfer document. Where flats are concerned you will be urged to conform since there will be other people in the block who will be declaring considerably less than you for an identical flat. But with a house or land you are best advised to pay the full rate of tax. Remember that everyone in Italy pays capital gains tax irrespective of whether it is a principal private residence or not or whether he is a foreigner or native. Moreover when a property owner dies it is often the local council's district surveyor who assesses the value of property for death duty purposes — then its market value is given and the inheritors pay duty on its real worth. It really does not pay to try to cheat the Revenue in Italy.

5 The buying process

In Italy as in England, buying property falls into two parts — the contract and the conveyance or *atto*. Essentially what is done in each country has the same object which is to see that you get what you agreed to buy, that it brings with it no surprises, that it serves the purpose for which it was sold to you and that you get a good title to it. The way in which the Italian system sets about this is rather different from the way it is done in Britain.

The contract

In Britain, when you have found the house you like, you tell the estate agent to send details to your solicitor and you pay him a visit. He gets in touch with the seller's solicitor who sends him a draft of the contract. He then makes enquiries and when he is satisfied with all the answers he gets and with what the contract says, he explains it all to you and recommends that you sign it. The seller then signs his part of the contract and the deal is done.

This is not the way it happens in Italy. The normal procedure is for the seller's estate agent to prepare the contract, known as a *compromesso* or *promessi di vendità* which are often in standard, even printed, form and hand it to the buyer for signature. The Italian buyer frequently signs without question if the price is right and the date for completion is satisfactory. This can be a terrible mistake since the purchaser is allowed by law to make all sorts of conditions to such a contract not least that he gets a required loan or that, if it is building land, he hands over no money until such time as he has a *licenza* which has at least two years to run, in his hand. In some cases, no great harm is done by following the estate agent's and vendor's wishes if you are buying a flat in one of the large cities but even so you should always put in a clause about getting a loan.

Signature and deposits

Except in the case of building land you pay a ten per cent deposit based on the asking price. However, if you are buying land or any kind of property particularly in the country, you should always get advice before signing anything. People are not beyond selling land for building which will never get planning permission. Moreover planning permission **can lapse** in Italy and you should carefully note the expiry date. Until you have either a *licenza* with two years to run or have a new *licenza* for three years sign nothing and hand over no money.

An Italian lawyer, *geometrà* or *commercialistà* will be able to help and most will redraw the contract for you putting in your conditions. This is not to say that the vendor will accept all your conditions since he too can refuse to sign but usually there are no problems unless you stipulate the impossible.

Once such a contract has been signed by both parties it is binding. A purchaser who cannot complete loses his deposit. A vendor who cannot complete must pay you back **double** your deposit within a given time limit fixed by the contract. If he does not agree to do this then it is achieved by negotiation or ordered by a court. It is to be hoped that it will not come to court as it can then take ages to settle. This is why it is essential to have the full asking price on this first document.

Agents and commission

It is not unusual for agents to prepare contracts without ever having seen the title deeds of the property in question. Indeed, it is rare that they have seen the title deeds. This means that the property you are buying may be wrongly described and important details may be missing. This is bad enough with a flat in a block but in the case of country properties and land itself, this is dangerous. A full description should appear and except in the simplest cases, you should insist on a cadastral plan. Where you are buying land, about which there seems some doubt, it does not come amiss to employ a surveyor (*geometrà*) to mark the boundaries for you in consultation with your neighbours thus scotching any quarrels in the future.

If you are buying land which was part of a greater parcel or parcels of land a survey **must** be done prior to completion and the new title registered separately at the provincial land registry (*catasto*). It is the vendor who pays for this service by a *geometrà* and it rarely costs less than one and a half to two million lire.

Always pay the deposit to the notary, who is acting for you (he will be acting for the vendor as well), and never to the estate agent. Most Italian estate agents are honest but the calling seems to attract some crooks as well so be very circumspect about money matters. One unpleasant habit that a very few estate agents seem to have is to sell property at several million lire more than the asking price by the vendor, pocket the difference by way of commission and charge the percentage commission legally due from the purchaser (around two per cent) on the asking price whilst at the same time the vendor is busy declaring via the notary only a small percentage of **his** asking price.

Watch the clause about commission. In all parts of Italy, agent's commission is shared by seller and buyer. The rates vary from one region to another and are set by the local

Chamber of Commerce (*Camera di Commercio*). It is a good idea to check the rate of commission and the percentage paid by both the vendor and the purchaser. The purchaser usually pays less than the vendor. The agent is concerned to see himself paid. The percentage commission can vary but usually it is five per cent of which the purchaser pays two per cent and the seller three per cent. Make certain that the reference to commission in the contract does not impose a joint liability ie that failure of the seller to pay his three per cent obliges you to pay the full five per cent.

Unlike many West European countries Italian notaries are not allowed to sell property and are not allowed to charge commission. The Italian notary is probably the most tightly controlled public officer there is and yet you will never get a 'statement of account' at the end of your purchase showing his fees etc. His fees are set by the government and are on a descending scale. Once you know how much the stamp duty is you can make an inspired guess as to how much he has charged you. He is never questioned by the government because he declares the scale fee plus VAT. Most notaries do not charge VAT except on the scale part of the fee — which is why they will not give you a statement of their charges. As in the UK it is a heinous crime to charge VAT and not give it to the government and it incurs greater penalties than merely not paying income tax on a fee. If found to be taking VAT and not passing it over to the government there is no question of a fine — the person goes to jail unless it can be proved it is a genuine error.

Completion dates and enquiries

It is rare for completion dates to be fixed six weeks in advance and they are usually on an 'on or before' basis. This is to your advantage since the Italian administrative system is not sound enough to be certain that any searches and enquiries will come back in time. Such enquiries and searches will only be made for you by the person you employ to advise you — it will not be done automatically by the notary whose main job is to transfer the property and see the taxes are paid. If you do use the notary for making searches and enquiries he will require a small extra payment for this service but you should always ask him to do this for you if you have no one else working on your behalf. Provided he reports to you the result of his searches under his personal signature he then becomes liable to you for anything he may have omitted to communicate. This potential delay can mean your deposit cheque is lying around for rather a long time. Legally it can be encashed by the vendor or can be held on his behalf by either the notary or the estate agent but can not be encashed by either of them. No notary in Italy has an account which is the same or similar to a solicitor's 'Clients' Account'.

Most searches are made after the *compromesso* has been signed so that they tend to be subject to rather general conditions that nothing ghastly or impossible will turn up. In virtually all parts of Italy such searches have to be made in person by the purchaser or his notary, Italian lawyer or *geometrà*. Generally, property is sold subject to the condition that it is taken in the state it is on completion. What happens between contracts and completion needs watching and it is as well to state as one of **your** conditions that certain fittings are not to be removed or damaged.

If what is being bought is in a condominium or part of a divided property a copy of the last service charge account should be asked for. Newer blocks of flats usually have a large book of rules and regulations governing what can and cannot be done and if this exists it is essential you have a copy of it before finally signing the *atto*. It is irrelevant whether you read Italian or not since the vendors are required to obtain this document and hand it over to the purchaser.

Trusts

Trusts as they are known in the UK are not wholly understood by the Italians and the tendency is, therefore, to treat trustees as though they were the real owners of the property. There are certain *fondazioni* (see Glossary) which are run by what in the UK would be called trustees but these are on a very large scale and are usually charities. They require separate permission from both the Italian Revenue and from the Italian Parliament to obtain this status. Hardly something the average British purchaser should involve himself in.

Company purchases

Buying a property via a non-Italian company is something that should be discussed with both your UK accountant and an Italian *commercialistà*. There may be some advantages to be gained, such as not paying almost 18% stamp duty on the transfer of land in Italy since it can be effected by a transfer of the shares and it may be possible to obviate paying Italian inheritance tax. However, in certain circumstances the Italian tax authorities may try to treat the shareholders as direct owners of the property and charge inheritance tax accordingly.

There is another reason for not buying a property in this way and that is that it excludes its resale to most Italians since, at the moment, they cannot buy shares in a foreign company unless they are permanently resident out of Italy. Even those persons returning to live in Italy will have to regularize the position and pay full stamp duty on the transfer to their own name. This means that your future buyer will have to be a non-Italian. For an ordinary house or flat it is hardly worth the trouble though, of course, in the case of a vineyard or large agricultural undertaking, known as an *azienda agricola* it may well have great tax advantages.

The conveyance

Once the contract (*compromesso* or *promessi di vendità*) has been signed the vendor and the purchaser have committed themselves both to a future signing of the conveyance, known as the *atto* for the transfer of the property from one to the other and to the payment of taxes, notably INVIM, a form of capital gains tax chargeable on the sale of **every** property in Italy, by the vendor and the payment of stamp duties and notary's fees by the purchaser. This *atto* is then registered at the local land registry and a copy is sent to Rome for fiscal purposes.

The *Numero di Codice Fiscale*

Everyone in Italy who purchases property will have been issued with a special number known as a *Numero di Codice Fiscale*. Thereafter, every large purchase such as a car, gas or oil for central heating, boats, domestic appliances or a mink coat will incur your giving them your *Codice Fiscale* number. If you merely come to Italy on a holiday basis and own nothing in Italy, you will not be asked for this number. However if you buy a house in Italy for holidays you will be issued with one by the local tax office. This is done very quickly and you can acquire it on the morning of the day you sign the conveyance. You should remember that Italian Government Offices, including the Tax Office, are only open in the mornings until 1.20 pm. You will not need this number when you sign the contract. Such numbers can also be issued to companies (both Italian and non-Italian) as well as private individuals.

It is worth mentioning that if you become resident and insist on false tax declarations, there is a computerised record in

Rome of every large purchase you have made. Thus there is no point in declaring 12 million lire as your income when you have spent 20 million on purchases during the year. One day two and two may well be put together. It is a chance not worth taking.

What does the conveyance consist of?

The appearance of the Italian *atto* always comes as a shock to foreigners. Everything is typed out on *carta bollata* which has lines. This came about because stamp duty was (and still is) charged per page and in the old days Italians used to stamp large sheets of paper with the relevant excise duty stamp and cram hundreds of tiny lines of very small writing or typing onto it. Now every piece of *carta bollata* has the same measurements and is lined in accordance with government requirements so no cheating can occur.

The *atto* will recite the names, dates of birth and addresses of both the vendor and purchaser and will give the exact location and size of the property being transferred using the cadastral plans and its lot numbers. It will name your immediate neighbours and their lot numbers which have a boundary with your property. It is by no means standard practice to give a recital of the previous title. Usually the vendor or his immediate predecessor will be all that is mentioned.

The vendor will give an undertaking that all mortgages and loans on the property have been paid or will be paid. However, it is as well to get your notary or adviser to check at the local mortgage registry just what remains on the record and then re-check in a couple of months that they have been removed. Irrespective of the owner, the mortgage remains on the property until it has been paid off.

This is the vendor's duty and if it has not been paid off within two or three months you will have to instruct a lawyer to make sure it is. Since the vendor has made the statement in the *atto* that he has, or will do this, the costs of forcing him to do so are for his account, not yours. Alternatively and preferably, one of the conditions in your contract should be that he pays off all mortgages and loans on the property prior to conveying it to you. Sometimes this is a little difficult to arrange since he will need the proceeds of sale to do so. If so, you can then put in a condition that you will hand over the amount due for the mortgage to either the notary or your adviser for **him** to pay off the mortgage. The best way is, of course, to insist on the condition that the land is totally free of mortgages and loans at the time of transfer to you. Once the contract has been signed the vendor can get a short term bridging loan to pay off such debts. Unfortunately, such an idea does not appeal to most Italians and given the rates of interest in Italy one cannot always blame them.

Completion

As a buyer attempting to deal with a purchase on your own, it is highly improbable that you will hear anything until you receive from the notary, probably pushed by the vendor, a letter giving you a date for completion (probably without any words of explanation). You will not, as in Britain, be advised from time to time of progress. The notary may assume that you are coming in person to complete or he may assume that you are appointing an attorney. The rule is that all parties to a notarial document must be present in person or be represented by an attorney for the entire duration of the proceedings.

Those who are single, divorced or widowed obviously do not need to produce a marriage certificate but married persons most certainly do. If only one party to a marriage buys property then it is assumed that he or she was married under the matrimonial regime of *separazione dei beni* (see Glossary). Moreover, on the sale of property, married persons, whatever their nationality, need to produce a certificate issued by the Italian Consulate of their country stating whether matrimonial regimes exist or not. In the UK they do not and you will find that unless you have a certificate from the Italian Consulate you will not be able to transfer the property. If a husband and wife have bought jointly they will sell jointly so the problem of furnishing a consular certificate will not arise. However, if you are married it is always best to have your marriage certificate with you.

The best way for married persons to buy is in joint names with the surviving husband or wife having a life interest in the property. Children pay very low inheritance tax in Italy but husbands or wives pay rather more. There is no problem of Italian law affecting your purchase. You can leave your property to whom you wish though you should bear in mind that inheritance tax is paid by the beneficiary according to his relationship to the deceased. The deceased's children pay the lowest of all. It is important to remember that there is no surviving spouse exemption from inheritance tax in Italy.

Of course, if you are not in the country and have asked a local professional person to act on your behalf, he will have been watching over things and keeping you posted and in due course will send you a power of attorney or act on the one you have already given him.

Power of Attorney

To make a Power of Attorney in the Italian form you will need an accurate description of the property you are buying, an accurate description of the purchasers and you should get either your own Italian lawyer or the notary to draw one up for you. This Power of Attorney can be signed in front of an Italian notary if you are in Italy in which case you need do nothing more.

Alternatively, you can sign a Power of Attorney previously prepared by an Italian notary before the Italian Consul nearest to your home in the UK in which case you will need your birth certificate, your passport to prove your citizenship, your marriage certificate, if you have one, and full details of the property to be conveyed to you or by you. You will also need to furnish some proof of identity of the person to whom you are giving the power. Many of the larger and more important Italian Consulates have ready printed forms for powers of attorney and all you have to do is supply the necessary information. However, do not rely on this form being available — always ask beforehand.

Finally you can sign an Italian Power of Attorney before a Notary Public in your nearest town but you should remind him that such a document needs a Hague Convention Apostille added to it, or his signature can be legalised by the Italian Consul. Without the Hague Convention Apostille or legalisation by the Italian Consulate, the Power of Attorney will be useless in Italy. It is really best to use a Notary Public in London or the local Italian Consulate (who obviously does not need an Apostille). Using the Italian Consulate to legalise the signature of a Notary Public in England can take a very long time and is not a recommended method. It is best to arrange that the Notary Public himself obtains the Apostille and to refuse it if it has not got this addition.

A fee and stamp duty are payable for a Power of Attorney **wherever you have it done**. It is **never** included in the notarial fees.

The amount required on completion will include notarial fees, stamp duties and other disbursements. There is no 'completion statement' in the English sense of the term. Such costs must be paid **on or before completion**. No problems arise on the registration of the conveyance to you. This is undertaken by the notary forthwith since he is bound to pay over the taxes within a given period. Your conveyance is filed at the local provincial *catasto* or land registry but this guarantees nothing and is merely an archive for documents. This should not upset a future purchaser since there are very few problems about questions of possession in Italy.

Rights of way

One of the most important things to look for on the purchase document is easements, particularly those known as *servitù di passagio* or rights of way. There are two sorts of easements in Italian law, temporary, ie for 20 years at a time after which it needs to be renewed and those which are perpetual. If a neighbour has a right of way over your land since March 1971 he will need to renew it in March 1991. If he does not the easement lapses and you can, in theory, refuse to let him pass. This is the same for those who have access to your well or water source — if it is not perpetual it must be renewed every 20 years.

Watch out for people who consistently use your property as a short cut since before you know where you are they will have claimed and registered a legal right of way. Seven years is the normal period to claim a right of way and if you are a newcomer you will be told by the interested party that he has been using it for six and a half! If he insists on continuing to use it despite your instructions to the contrary consult your lawyer. Italians will try anything on foreigners including picking their olives, fruit, flowers, lavender etc on the grounds that they and their families have been doing this for donkeys' years. Behave exactly as an Italian would (with whom they would never try to pull such a fast one) and either scream at them to go away or find the relevant document to support your case (if this fails threaten them with the *carabinieri*, which always frightens them).

However, there is a type of easement in Italy which you are bound to continue or give. This is an easement of necessity or *servitù di necessità*. A typical example would be where your land cut off access to your neighbour's property and the only way to it was across your land. These are nearly always very obvious and are usually registered. If the necessity is there you cannot, under any circumstances, refuse to allow your neighbour, his family and friends access to his property.

A word of warning

There are occasionally problems with property which does not officially exist. Where in Spain you could find yourself having bought a tract of land in the country which did not exist this could never happen in Italy if only because not a great deal changes hands in the country and when it does it is accompanied by a vast amount of documents. It is in the large towns where such fraud exists and particularly, with **large** blocks of flats where the builder has illegally built on another floor or a couple of other flats for which he had no permission. By dint of bribery or some other jiggery-pokery he has managed to get all the rest of the building passed by the local authority or alternatively, he has built on at a later date.

Never, never buy any property which is offered to you by way of shares in an Italian company without consulting your own Italian lawyer. Of course there are many flats owned perfectly legally by Italian companies but it is always a good idea to check **the property** as well as the company before buying and only an Italian professional adviser is capable of doing so.

Never buy property where the vendor says there is no need to involve a notary! It may seem incredible that one has to say this but there are people tempted by a top floor flat in Milan at a knock down price who can easily be bamboozled by the vendor handing over his service charge accounts which show the flat as part of the *condominio*. Stop and think for a moment. Why should this flat have the use of the lift, entrance, common parts of the building and perhaps central heating and hot water without paying some contribution? A block of flats, known as a *condominio* in Italian, is not a charitable institution. Remember also, you can never get a loan on such property since officially it does not exist and the bank or lending institution cannot take a charge on non-existent property. Imagine trying to sell such a property in the future. If ever, at some time in the future the block is the subject of a compulsory purchase order you will receive no compensation for your penthouse — nor will a property company think of purchasing your flat when redevelopment of the site is in issue.

Finally it is worth remembering that you, as the so-called proprietor in residence, may well find your property can be demolished before your eyes **without any compensation** by the local authority or you may be landed with a huge fine known as a *condono edilizio* (or worse still both).

Such properties represent a microscopic proportion of what is on sale in Italy and since there is plenty of property which can be conveyed legally it is not necessary for a foreigner to dabble in this kind of market.

6 Buying land

Every square centimetre of land in Italy is ostensibly zoned as either building land, farming land, olive groves, forest or sea-shore; the last three of which will never get their status changed.

Most of the provincial land registries are years behind in their maps and frequently new roads or buildings have appeared on the scene but not on the map. However, the local *comune* in which the land is situate will have considerably more up to date maps.

Although you may be allowed to build in an olive grove you will not be allowed to cut down more olive trees than the *comune* tells you and if you do and are found out, the fines can be enormous.

Even if a forest belongs to you it is unlikely you will be allowed to build in it, but if you are you will be hedged by all sorts of rules and regulations. In the drier parts of Italy it can be a positive danger being in the middle of a forest due to the numerous forest fires each summer. You will be required, as are all property owners in the country, to keep your land clean and the grass and undergrowth cut short to avoid fires. Unlike in France where if you do not do this the State Forestry Department will do it for you and charge a fortune, the Italians will simply impose a fine on you for having left your property in a state where fire can take hold, thus adding insult to injury. In some parts of Italy you will be obliged to have fire ditches dug and cleared out each year — an excellent idea which can prevent catastrophe. Some insurance companies will also require you to make your land as fire-proof as possible. During certain months of the year fires are forbidden throughout Italy though you would not always know it. However, if a garden bonfire does get out of control you are bound for trouble with the local fire service and again a fine is in the offing. Therefore, it pays to take as many precautions as possible **for your own sake** if living in the countryside or a forest.

No-one is allowed to build within 300 metres of the sea-shore anywhere in Italy and it is hoped by this regulation to stop some of the awful building speculation which has gone on in places like Rapallo.

Density regulations

Every *comune* throughout Italy has a Zoning Commission known as a *Commissione Edilizia* and they decide within certain limits imposed by the province or region what may or may not be built and where. There are density regulations, ie so many cubic metres for so many square metres of land and often there are zones, such as in the town itself where the density allowances are greater. Often a *comune* will have as many as four different zones.

Zone (a) will be in the centre of the *comune* where, since land is at a premium you will be able to have more cubic metres per square metre of land. However, almost certainly, you will be hedged in by building regulations which do not necessarily apply elsewhere, such as not being allowed to use metal shutters or windows, having to face your property in the old stone of the area or not being allowed to erect a wall round your garden for the sake of privacy.

Zone (b) will be just outside the centre and you will require more land to get the same size house.

Zone (c) will be the same thing only more so — you will need a great deal of land to get a decent sized house.

Zone (d) will be land zoned as agricultural on which nothing, except greenhouses and agricultural sheds and barns can be built. The only entity which can overrule such zoning is the Italian state and occasionally an army or Carabinieri barracks will be built in this zone. Such occurrences are few and far between.

Density regulations are set every five or ten years depending on the local *comune*. Thus you may find that persons living in Zone (b) will be able to increase their house by as much as 50% ten years later on. Normally the amounts are increased by between 20 to 25%. The central zone rarely has its density regulations changed since they are crowded enough already.

Occasionally you will see a large house on a small parcel of land and will wonder how that came about since it is obvious the density regulations have not been observed. The answer is simple, though complicated in execution. That person either has land elsewhere in the *comune* which is zoned for building and which has either not been built on at all or has not used up its full volume entitlement. Alternatively he has purchased from someone else who has unused building land in the same *comune* the right to build and he can now use it on his own land. Once the building right on land has been sold the land becomes zoned for agricultural purposes and can never be built on. The owner keeps the land but cannot develop it.

This sort of undertaking must be dealt with by a qualified Italian architect or *geometrà* and it has to be done via an Italian notary. There is a fee to be paid to the land owner for the transfer of the right and a fee and stamp duty to the notary. Never, never pay out money until your architect or *geometrà* informs you that the necessary permission has been given via a **letter from the comune** (word of mouth or verbal promises just will not do) and never listen to an Italian who suggests, as is quite possible, that such a small thing need not go through the notary. Without notarial proof that you own the right to build you will not be able to build more than the amount your parcel of land is zoned for.

Building regulations

One thing that upsets newcomers to many parts of Italy is the ostensibly unsuitable land which is offered for sale as building plots. Much Italian land is terraced and requires very specialised building procedures, particularly so far as foundations and septic tanks are concerned. You must remember that Italians have been building on this type of land for centuries; indeed in some areas there is often **only** this type of land for building on. The building techniques are very different in much of Italy. Reinforced concrete structures are commonly used, particularly in earthquake zones, and often roofs are solid concrete with tiles stuck on to make it look more conventional than it is.

Every region or *comune* has its own building regulations. You are unlikely to be able to build a Venetian Palladio type villa in Liguria or an Abbruzzese tower house in the Veneto. By and large you must build in the local style. Therefore, as well as looking for the climate which you think will suit, you should look also at the local style of building. If you don't think much of it perhaps you should move on to somewhere where the local architecture is more beautiful. Do not go too much by what the centre of a town looks like. Too often it is exaggeratedly old and beautiful or too modern and industrial and what you will be able to build outside will be much more to your taste. As in the UK so in Italy. Very often beautiful countryside seems to produce rather boring architecture as if the view were enough whereas places with rather flat and boring countryside seem to have wonderful architecture. Parts of the Veneto are flat and covered in endless vineyards yet the architecture is among the best in Italy.

7 Building a new property

The basic rules

If you finally decide to build your own house in Italy there are certain basic rules to be followed.

First you must have a plot of land or be about to purchase a plot of land **which has already got planning permission or is zoned for building**. Pay nothing to the owner of the plot and sign nothing until this planning permission, known as a *licenza* is issued. If there is already planning permission granted for the land then make sure it has at least two years to run. Italian planning permission can last from between one to three years. The date on the planning permission *licenza* is very important indeed.

Secondly you will need an architect or a surveyor, *geometrà*, to draw up plans for you and submit them to the local planning authority of your *comune*. Usually this is done before you commit yourself to buying the land — the planning permission is issued on the basis of your architect's drawings. There will be a fee to pay to the architect and to the *comune* for the permission which varies from one part of Italy to another but nowadays will never be less than three million lire for the average 100 square metre house. Architects charge between five per cent and ten per cent on the cost of the building but this will include supervision of the works from beginning to end.

Thirdly you will need to find a builder (usually via the architect or *geometrà*) and establish a firm contract with him including penalty clauses for late completion. The architect or *geometrà* will know of plenty of builders and will be able to show you the sort of work they have done in the past.

Finally you must realise that come what may you will have to conform to the local style of building at least as far as the exterior is concerned. There are some *comuni* who even insist on certain colours or stone being used.

The *geometrà*

Whether you choose a *geometrà* or architect is up to you — they do much the same sort of job though many people find that a *geometrà* is a more practical sort of man than an architect.

Incidentally, if you are restoring and extending an old property you will still need planning permission and probably a *geometrà* is a better person to employ to survey the property in the first place and to produce drawings for its restoration.

Planning regulations

Planning regulations are probably as tight in Italy as in the UK and if you do something not previously passed you may well be forced to demolish it (at your expense), pay a fine or both. The fine can become so great that the building can be taken from you and sold to raise the proceeds. Never listen to an Italian who tells you that you can pay a small fine and get back-dated building permission, or *condono edilizio*, for having done work before you got permission. It is a very dangerous pastime and unless you actually enjoy gambling is one that can give sleepless nights. It is not a method to be recommended.

The Building Committee

Your plans are presented at the next meeting of the Building Committee or *Commissione Edilizia* of the *comune* in which the house is going to be built. They must be accompanied by an accurate map of where the plot is, together with drawings for drainage and septic tanks. If there is to be a swimming pool a separate septic tank will be needed. Very often local builders in the village are members of this committee and it can be quite useful if your builder (or his father, brother, cousin etc) is on it. It is not necessary but it helps. Once passed, your project, known as a *progetto*, will be issued with a number. The *comune* will shortly thereafter issue a building permit or *licenza* and you or your architect or *geometrà* must go to the *comune*'s offices (*municipio*) to sign for it. Although typed up and ready it cannot be used until it has your (or your architect's) signature on it.

Services

All the boring things like having water, site electricity, drainage etc you can now safely leave to the architect to deal with. Occasionally he will come to you for the odd signature and your presence will be required at their offices in the nearest town in order to have ENEL, the nationalised electricity board, survey the building and connect the permanent electricity.

Italians are second to none in bathroom and kitchen design but it is as well to choose exactly the kitchen and sanitary ware **you** want before drawing up the building contract. Remember that the standard height of Italian kitchen units can be rather low for North Europeans and these units may well need to be put on a higher plinth than normal.

Other things to remember are that if you are in the country you will need a special sort of water pump to get sufficient pressure to make the water-heaters function properly. This is known as an *autoclave* and is usually essential out of built up areas. Also watch the contract for clauses about things like tiling the garage, cellar and utility room floors, since lots of Italians leave them as bare cement and you may not want this, construction of proper paths to the house and garage — this is frequently left out of contracts — and making good any terraces which have been destroyed by earth moving machinery since this can be horrifically expensive and messy once the builders have gone. If the garden is large and earth moving equipment is used it is probably the moment to put in either automatic underground irrigation systems or low stand pipes for clipping on hoses.

Still on the subject of water do make sure that rain water can be drained well away from the house. In much of Italy, rain is heavy and much of it 'runs-off' doing little good to the garden unless you can arrange to collect it in large tanks for future use.

Design

You must decide from the outset whether you want a balcony or balconies and terraces on your house — they are expensive to build on at a later date. Be very careful where you site your terrace. Much time in Italy is spent out of doors and you must be careful not to have a terrace where the wind blows all the time.

Because of the immense summer heat **all** houses and flats need some form of shutter. These are traditional in Italy (and vary from one part to the other) and keep out the extremes of weather. The only alternative to shutters is a special type of glass which screens out the dangerous rays of the sun — this is very expensive and not always successful.

The Italians make a brilliant combination of double-glazed window, shutter and mosquito net which folds back invisibly behind the shutter in the day time. They come in anodized or plain aluminium and in any colour.

Heating and insulation

British people are always amazed at where the Italians (except in north east Italy) choose to put their fireplaces — usually in a corner which allows one or at most two people to get near it. Fireplaces are strictly decorative in Italy — the central heating is for heating so if you want a proper, large fireplace you must specify this in advance. Anywhere north of Rome, and even there at times, needs central heating. In the north it can become very, very cold in winter except on the coast. This brings one to another sore subject in Italy, insulation or *isolazione*.

Italian builders and architects can be very slaphappy and mean with insulation. Unlike France, there are few special types of plasterboard which have a thick insulating layer in the middle. However, glasswool, polystyrene, special foams, etc, are all known in Italy. When you see your insulation clause get the architect to double the thickness stated. Doubtless, he will say it is not necessary but you are paying both for the building and the future heating bills and twice the thickness of insulation will pay dividends in the future. If you do have metal windows they are not so very much more expensive if double-glazed, which keeps out cold, heat and noise. At the right time go on site and **check** the thickness of insulation, since they may well have thought you mad and will have taken no notice of you.

Even if you do not use it for water heating in the house it is worth considering solar-heating if you have a swimming pool. Used in conjunction with a heat-exchanger it can be a very economical way of heating a pool. It is also quite useful for heating water in spare bathrooms which are mainly used in summer when you have guests staying. For everyday use it can turn out to be expensive in Italy since its use is combined with an electric immersion heater which will incur putting in at least another phase. Heating water by electricity is an expensive method in Italy. There are no cheap times and no white meters.

Workmanship

Italian workmanship, particularly in plastering, tiling and wood can be the best in the world. Anyone who has seen a properly tiled Italian floor will vouch for that. However, **you** will need to go and choose tiles — never leave it to the architect or builder and you may well need to go to several showrooms before you find what you want. As in Spain, after the UK, tiles seem very cheap in Italy and so is marble and granite which are used for fireplaces, window sills, door and window surrounds, toppings for pilasters etc. Never have a marble or granite staircase though which can be a death trap in wet weather. Alas, finding the proverbial brilliant Italian builder is not always easy. It is best to ask to see some of his previous work — he should be thrilled to show it to you and Italians **never** mind showing off their house and giving you a glass of wine whilst doing it.

Alternatives to building your own home

An alternative to building a house yourself is to buy a partially built one or a flat in the course of construction. With the first you will have a great deal of choice where the interior is concerned but with the latter you will find you are much more limited.

In flats, to save room presumably, the Italians have recently become enthusiastic about open-plan kitchens, dining rooms and living rooms. If it can be avoided so much the better — except for really powerful extractors over the cooker very few cooker hoods work really well.

All the same planning rules apply except that there will already be (one hopes!) a *licenza* for the work in hand. Nearer the time for completion of the work it is a good idea to have a *geometrà* examine the property and tell you what is missing, if anything, and how certain shortcomings can be put right. Have a survey done in fact. It will cost very little considering the peace of mind it will give you.

Payment

There will be stage payments to make to the builder as the work progresses. If it is a flat these will be laid out in a document — so many per cent at such and such a stage. Virtually all blocks of flats in Italy in the course of construction have a bank guarantee and the stage payments will be worked out in conjunction with the bank.

For a house you pay the builder only on an architect's or *geometrà*'s certificate that a certain stage has been reached. There is no reason why you should take on the old contract with the builder exactly, with just the name of the owner changed. You should negotiate a new contract with the help of an architect or lawyer and make sure there are penalties for late delivery.

All new building work in Italy is subject to 19% IVA (VAT). If the builder approaches you to pay him less and forget about the IVA do not listen. Your contract must be registered and have stamp duty paid on it (a very small amount) and you must pay IVA at 19% or you will end up with a capital gains tax bill (INVIM) of up to 30% on resale.

It is false economy as well as illegal to cheat on IVA on new buildings.

On selling the property you will need to produce evidence of everything you have spent on building the house. Unless the bills carry full IVA they will not be admitted. Therefore, if you pay 120 million lire to build a house and have nothing to show for it (a) the registry and the Ministry of Finance will know you have cheated and (b) you will pay around 40 million lire to the state in capital gains tax (INVIM) and probably a fine as well.

The examination

Before being allowed to live in your new property it must be examined by the local provincial engineer to see if it is properly built. This is called a *collaudo* or examination. He will test the strength of reinforced concrete, the square metrage of the property and its volume — so no cheating on size. This will cost between 200,000 and 300,000 lire. Once the *collaudo* has been issued a habitation certificate (*certificato d'abitazione*) is issued by the *municipio* (town hall). Both these documents should be kept carefully and handed on to anyone who buys it from you.

In the case of a block of flats the whole block will be subject to a *collaudo* and the cost of this will be passed on to you either separately or in the price of the property. A habitation certificate will be granted by the local *municipio* or there may be a general one for the whole block. The *geometrà* who surveys the finished flat will be able to tell you which applies. Although you will have been allotted a meter for both water and electricity and perhaps gas if in town, this does not mean you will be automatically connected. You will need to go to the local offices and fill in various forms before they will do so. You need to be able to tell them exactly on which floor, which staircase and which side of the staircase your flat is. If it has a lot number so much the better. The electric installation as well as the gas will have been examined earlier and you will not need to arrange this.

8 Life in a condominium

The condominium is, of course, virtually unknown in England. A few are gradually being introduced. It would be a great pity if it were allowed to take over from the existing English system of buying a flat by taking a long lease from the owner of the block or taking over the lease from an existing flat owner. The Italian system which on the whole does not work as well as it could, just has to be accepted because there is no alternative. The one advantage which it has over some other systems is that the rules and regulations which govern the management of an Italian condominium must abide by the basic Italian law on the subject so that neither developers nor the flat owners themselves can make rules which are unreasonably restrictive or unfair.

The Italian system

You must appreciate the basic differences between the Italian and the British systems. What is known as a *condominio* in Italian becomes necessary only when there are five or more co-proprietors in the block. If the figure is lower than that you can make arrangements between yourselves. Thereafter, you will have to turn the building into a condominium and have an administrator, known in Italian as an *amministratore.* There is no need to be alarmed by this but if you do not learn this simple lesson, you will never be a happy flat-owner. In the UK, the usual scheme of things is for each flat owner to own his own flat but not to have any interest in the common parts of the block — the roof, the staircases, the drains etc. In Italy you own your flat but in addition you have an actual share in all the common parts of the block, the surrounding land, the swimming pool etc (known in Italian as the *ente condominiale*).

Under a British long lease of a flat, you have a whole list of obligations to your landlord. Your landlord probably has very many less towards you but they will include maintaining the block in exchange for which you pay a service charge. In Italy you have no landlord. You have a similar list of obligations and the liability to pay a service charge. In Britain, therefore, you have a number of flat-owners on the one hand very often represented by a tenants' association and a landlord (or possibly a management company) on the other. In Italy, the hand of every flat owner is turned against every other flat owner and the Italians can be rather demanding of each other.

In Britain, English is spoken. In Italy, Italian is spoken and everything to do with a condominium, its rules, its management and the part you should play in that is in Italian. This is part of 'being abroad' but help is nearly always close at hand.

Finally, you must get used to the fact that the ownership of a flat in Italy is neither freehold nor leasehold. That need not cause you any worry for you can still freely sell it, let it, mortgage it, give it away or leave it by Will. Imagine it as a freehold which has no land attached to it and you will not be far out.

Rules of the condominium

Before you contemplate the purchase of a flat, ideally you should ask the existing owner for a copy of his last service charge account as well as a copy of the rules of the condominium, known in Italian as *Regolamento del*

Condominio. These rules have the force of law in Italy and seriously breaking them can have unpleasant consequences. However, it is rare to find any rules which are unreasonable. You may well find that in the case of an 'old' flat, it will not be forthcoming and in the case of a new flat, it will be said that a copy will come along before completion. Desirable though it is to see this document as early as possible (most of them are drawn up by notaries) it is not a disaster if you cannot. If and when you do manage to lay hands on a copy you will find that it also contains the division of the block into *unità immobiliari* (see Glossary) giving each *unità* its share in the common parts of the block. Such shares are usually expressed as fractions of 1,000 and reflect the size and position of the flat in the block. This rule book will also contain:

- The share of service charges attributed to each flat owner.
- Rules about the calculation and payment of service charges.
- A long list of what each flat owner may and may not do.
- Rules applying to the management of the block.
- Rules applying to meetings of flat owners.
- A variety of rules dealing with such things as what happens if the block burns down, additions to the block are made, if it is desired to join two flats together etc.

Service charges

These may be divided into general and special charges. General charges will apply to expenses common to all flats; special charges are those applicable to individual blocks in a complex or, more unusually, to a flat or group of flats which enjoy an amenity which the others do not. Usually but not always, general charges will be the same proportion of the total general management expenses as your proportion of the common parts attaching to your flat. Usually, the proportion of service charges payable by a flat is not able to be altered.

Payment of service charges

These are based on an annual budget presented to the annual general meeting of the flat owners. It is customary to collect service charges half in arrears and half in advance. These advance payments are based on the budget and the final instalment in every year is a 'topping up' payment and sometimes is more than the half you had been expecting. Failure to pay service charges will result in the payment of interest and ultimately, of course, legal action. Service charge accounts are not easy to follow. The *amministratore* or managing agent should be prepared to explain them to you but some will and some will not. Some will explain them to you in such rapid machine-gun fire Italian you will be none the wiser. This is the moment to ask an Italian lawyer or a *geometrà* (who frequently is an *amministratore* himself) to check the accounts for you. If there are any anomalies he will soon sort them out for you. Alas, it is rare that there are mistakes. Mostly large service charges mean that some expensive project has to be undertaken as a matter of urgency. Frequently this can be due to central heating or hot water boilers which is why you should prefer flats with their own individual central heating and hot water.

What you may and may not do

In general terms, you may do anything you like inside your flat in the nature of decoration provided you do not interfere with any of the common parts of the building. You would be wise to discuss anything fundamental with the *amministratore* (see below) in case what you have in mind requires planning permission. Surprisingly small and minor things require planning permission as well as the permission of the *amministratore*. You must be careful with balconies and terraces where often what might seem to be part of your flat is in fact a common part of the building and this prevents you, for example, from repainting your terrace yourself.

You will certainly be required to conform to the standard type and pattern of exterior blinds and urged forcefully not to dry clothes on your balconies. This may seem incredible in Italy but clothes drying from windows and balconies are the sign of a poor *condominio*. Domestic animals are normally permitted without anyone's consent. Parking your car except in designated parking spaces is normally forbidden and since this is a rule which by tradition is ignored by visiting Italians to the vast annoyance of all, you are asked to uphold the British respect for rules and regulations by being obedient.

Overall insurance of the block is the responsibility of the condominium as a whole and forms part of your service charge. You will not be required to insure your flat but you would be mad not to do so. You should also make sure you get cover for renting another flat for a long period should your own flat burn down. Incidentally, if you require a reinforced door you must face it with the door belonging to the condominium and you must get the permission of the *amministratore* before you fit it. It will always be given with certain provisos.

You can, of course, use your flat only in accordance with the purposes permitted by the *amministratore* and this will normally be as a private dwelling house. However, mixed private and professional users are common in Italy and if you want to practise as a doctor or dentist or architect for example, from a flat it is quite probable that you will be allowed to do so. What you will not be able to do is run a hairdressing establishment or give noisy music lessons all day.

Management of the block

All the flat owners as a group form a council (*consiglio*) and appoint an *amministratore* to administer the property. Usually, his appointment is on a one year basis only but it can be for longer. Unfortunately, many *amministratori* fall far below the standard one could hope for and they do not form a profession which is held in great esteem in Italy. The *amministratore* is responsible to the condominium for its day to day management. He may be helped in this by a special committee chosen by the *consiglio*, the members of which are flat owners who are appointed annually. If there is such a committee, it will normally check the annual accounts of the *amministratore* but it is very rare that outside accountants are employed. Technically, everything that the *amministratore* does is open to inspection by flat owners. Since it is almost essential to have an *amministratore* available from the very beginning of a new development and there are at that time no flat-owners available to appoint him, it is usual for developers to appoint the first *amministratore* for subsequent approval by the flat owners. Unfortunately, subsequent flat owners seldom 'unappoint' him in time.

A good *amministratore* makes for a happy block. An inefficient *amministratore* is a disaster.

Meetings

This is the moment when flat owners can have their say. Certain unalterable rules apply to meetings:

- There must be at least one general meeting per year to approve accounts and the *amministratore*'s management for the past year, to pass the next year's budget, to (re-)appoint the *amministratore* for the next year and to deal with any other items put on the agenda either by the *amministratore* himself or at the prompting of a flat owner.
- There must be a quorum. This is 51% of the flat owners or their proxies. If this percentage is not obtained the meeting will be called for a week later. There are times when an *amministratore* prefers to have a small attendance and will call the next meeting for a time and day which he knows will not suit the majority! Then he can get necessary things done without having a large majority against him.

- Additional meetings can be called by the *amministratore* or requisitioned by flat owners but the proportion of flat owners needed to do this is sufficiently large to make certain that this rarely happens. In desperation you can send a letter, delivered personally by hand, to the other flat owners in the block and request a meeting that way.
- Depending on what was agreed by the first meeting of flat-owners between 15 and 30 days notice of meetings must be given by registered AR (recorded delivery) post. Notice posted to addresses out of Italy is unlikely to arrive in time for you to do much about the subjects on the agenda.
- Flat owners may attend meetings either personally or they may give a proxy to someone else to go instead of them. A proxy may act for only one flat owner at a time. Most condominiums allow anyone, whether he is a flat owner or not, to act as proxy but it is permitted to restrict him to being a co-owner. Neither the *amministratore* of the block nor any member of his family may act as a proxy.

Most usual questions are settled by a simple majority of votes. Certain resolutions such as the removal of an *amministratore* and building alterations need larger majorities and one or two need the consent of all the flat owners.

Meetings are usually chaired by a president, who is a member of the *consiglio*, and the *amministratore*. Meetings are usually long, noisy, frequently ill-tempered and indecisive. They are, of course, conducted in Italian.

Minutes of all meetings must be prepared and circularised to all flat owners. Minutes show who presided at the meeting, who was present, what were the resolutions on the agenda and whether they were passed or not. As is to be expected, the quality of the minutes can vary considerably.

Members absent from meetings

There is absolutely no requirement that any of the documents or proceedings of an Italian condominium should be in any language other than Italian. Unless you are reasonably fluent in Italian and able to be present at all meetings of a condominium you should in your own interest appoint a permanent proxy who conveniently could be your adviser in Italy. He will, quite reasonably charge a fee for attending meetings.

You may feel that your votes alone will achieve nothing. In a way, this is true but if all the flat owners who felt like that in fact turned up or were represented at meetings, a lot that goes by default might be properly dealt with, including the appointment of a new *amministratore* if the present one is not managing your block satisfactorily.

9 Timesharing

This does not exist in Italy for a multitude of reasons. The most important reason is that there is, at present, no legislation which governs such an ownership or part ownership and of course, this offers a great many opportunities for cheating both the people who buy timeshares and the Italian Inland Revenue.

There are one or two British companies who, from time to time, advertise timeshares in Italy — be very wary of such publicity. There is no way you can own a piece of Italian land, a flat or a villa for a mere two weeks a year. You will be making a private arrangement with the company and you will have no recourse under either Italian or English law.

There is really very little more to say except to avoid such an undertaking like the plague until Italian law provides protection for timeshare owners.

10 You and the Italian banks

Whether you are buying property in Italy for a permanent or a holiday home, it is almost inevitable that you will need a bank account in Italy or at least come into contact with the Italian banking system.

The merits of having an Italian bank account

It is in theory possible to do without a bank account and exist on Eurocheques and credit cards but it will not be many weeks before you realise that this is quite impractical. Particularly if you are in Italy on a holiday basis you will find it easier for your bank to pay your gas, electricity and telephone bills direct. On the other hand, it is by no means a good idea to close your UK bank account or let your UK credit cards lapse if you are living in Italy permanently. To maintain the former gives you a certain freedom of action and to keep the latter avoids your having to use Italian credit cards which require you to pay off the whole outstanding balance every month by direct debit from your Italian bank account, unless you make prior arrangements to pay off a percentage each month. This does not apply to Italian American Express or Diners Club cards where the total amount will be debited to your account each month.

Problems can be encountered with the Italian banks when one is trying to telex money **fast** to Italy. Sixteen days can be a good average since once the money leaves your bank it goes to its correspondent bank in Milan or Rome and gets stuck there for days. The average office worker in Italy is woefully underpaid and as a consequence, the efficiency of such offices leaves something to be desired. It becomes a vicious circle. The overall effect is that people often don't work very fast or very efficiently unless working for themselves. The best way to send money to Italy from the UK is by Swiftair using a draft drawn on an Italian bank **in Italy**. This is simple to arrange.

Exchange Control

Officially Italy still has Exchange Control though to all practical purposes it has disappeared. The Italian Exchange Control Authority is known as the *Ufficio Italiano dei Cambi* and it is this organisation which decides, through the local banks, whether a person is resident or not. There has never been any hard and fast rule about this and the matter is becoming less and less important. However, there are still limits set on how much, as a resident, you may take out at a time (this increases virtually every week) and when you may take out the proceeds of the sale of your home in Italy. If you pay tax in Italy, pay the resident rates for gas, electricity and telephone you are considered to be resident and bound by Italian exchange control rules. However, as a foreigner you can have bank accounts other than in Italy, without permission, and you can use these for travel out of Italy.

If you are non-resident ie spend less than 183 days a year in Italy, pay income tax elsewhere and do not qualify for a Residence Certificate from your local *municipio* then you can operate a number of different types of account all of which allow freedom of money in and out of the country. You are, as a foreign national, allowed to operate bank accounts anywhere in the world.

Until relatively recently no Italian resident could take his cheque book abroad, let alone use it there. The back of every cheque was clearly marked as being valid only in Italy. Today he can use his resident cheques more or less anywhere in Europe. All the rules are changing daily and the only one which still seems to be in force is that you may pay up to five million lire into your account in foreign currency without any customs declaration. Thereafter, you must provide a customs declaration showing the source of the funds.

Italian banks

Many of the famous Italian banks are known abroad such as Credito Italiano, Banca Commerciale Italiana, Nuovo Banco Ambrosiano and Banca d'America e d'Italia to name but a few. However, there are lesser known banks which are just as big such as Istituto Bancario di San Paolo di Torino or Banco di Roma. Virtually every province has its own savings bank usually called *Cassa di Risparmio di* somewhere or other such as Genoa, Tuscany or Emilia-Romagna, etc. One of the oldest banks in Italy is the *Monte dei Paschi di Siena* which was started centuries ago.

Opening an account

The formalities for opening an account in Italy are similar to those in the UK although a great deal more paper work is required. For a foreigner, the banks need a copy of your passport and a 'fiscal' address. This for the non-resident is your home in England or for the resident your home in Italy. On the whole, joint accounts have advantages, if only because on the death of one holder, the other can usually continue to draw.

Both current accounts and various types of deposit accounts exist. At the moment, interest on non-resident deposit accounts is paid free of Italian withholding tax but this advantage for the UK tax resident may disappear if certain EC proposed tax rules come into force in Italy. Such accounts are not shown to the Italian tax authorities unless, later on, you are involved in criminal activity.

Cheques and credit cards

As in the UK, Italians use open and crossed cheques but mostly the former. They can be endorsed over more than once though this is not advisable. Therefore, you can pay your gardener with a cheque which, because he has no bank account, he will take to the local grocer and get cash for it. In Italy this can also be done with Eurocheques though again it is not advisable unless you know the parties concerned very well. Italians are very trusting in such matters, often to their detriment. Italy is however fairly similar to the UK and Germany in its banking philosophy. Many Italian banks now have the British system for cashing cheques, where all the tellers can cash cheques and it is not necessary to queue up at a separate *cassa* or till.

The cheque guarantee card exists but cheques tend not to be welcomed in shops. If you cannot pay in cash, which they prefer, they ask for a credit card and Visa and Access/ Mastercard are preferred to American Express and Diners Club though all four are taken in virtually every good restaurant and hotel throughout Italy. The banks all issue their own credit cards under the aegis of Visa or Mastercard — Carta Si being the most well known in Italy.

You cannot give a postdated cheque; that is to say, you can give it but it will be cleared on the day of its presentation whatever may be the date shown on the cheque. What you can do, since the Italians are eminently reasonable is give them post-dated cheques and ask them not to present them before that date. They will usually oblige.

If words and figures on a cheque do not agree the cheque is either returned or the drawer is telephoned to confirm the figure. If a cheque is more than six months old, it will be treated as 'stale' and again the drawer will be asked if it is all right to pay. It is unlikely that the receiving bank will accept a cheque more than six months old. Ordinary cheques take considerably longer to clear than in the UK.

Bank statements

Bank statements are somewhat complex and give only cheque numbers. This coupled with the slowness of clearing cheques and the fact that the Italians are sometimes lax about paying in cheques means that you have to treat the balances shown on your statements with reserve. It is possible to get photocopies of paid cheques but not without a great deal of difficulty so you need to have a good reason for wanting it. If you do not live permanently in Italy, make certain that statements are sent to you in the UK and not to your Italian address. Italian bank statements are issued monthly or quarterly and it is up to you to decide, bearing in mind you pay more for monthly statements.

'Bouncing' cheques

Very special rules apply to 'bouncing' cheques. They are too complicated to set out in detail but it should be pointed out that there are three things in Italy that can make the most innocent account holder bounce a cheque inadvertently. These are bank charges which most Italian banks (though by no means all) charge to your account without any warning, though at sufficiently regular intervals so that after a few jolts you should see the trouble coming, the unknown quantity of a telephone bill paid by direct debit and finally, the *conguaglio* or final reckoning produced by ENEL (the Italian electricity board) in December and June. All these items can not only drain a bank account but actually put it in the red. Unless prior arrangements have been made no cheque will be met on an overdrawn account. Sometimes the bank will pay ENEL or SIP if it overdraws your account but not always. Failure to pay what is known as your *bolleta luce* or *bolleta telefono (SIP)* (your telephone bill) incurs immediate disconnection.

The consequences are dire if a non-resident account is involved and the local judicial authorities step in. If you overdraw without permission on a resident account then that is between you and the payee. If you bounce a cheque and do not meet it within 15 days the matter goes to court and you are posted in both the local newspapers and the Official Gazette as a bouncer. You may end up not being able to have a bank account.

Bank drafts

Bank drafts are used particularly when you want to send or bring money from abroad. They are always given a value date but provided they are drawn on a well-known bank (foreign or Italian) you will probably be able to draw against it at once. Do not be surprised though to see later on that you have been charged overdraft interest — technically, because of a later value date you were in debit to the bank when it gave you cash for the draft.

The Italians also issue a form of certified cheque known as an *assegno circolare* for which the charge is minimal. This is the sort of cheque you use when buying a house, car or paying the notary his fees. Remember that although it may be made out to someone it is as good as cash and so its loss would be disastrous. You can also get your bank to credit the account of the garage, notary or vendor (providing you are given all the account details) and the receipt issued by the bank, known as a *tagliando*, will be accepted as evidence of payment. Most people who live in Italy for some time find the *assegno circolare* a very useful banking tool.

Direct debits

This is extremely useful in the case of electricity or gas or telephone bills since it avoids your arriving home only to find no light or no telephone. The bank simply pays but does not check. You will be sent direct a copy of the account. Check it but do not in your enthusiasm try and pay it again since you will find the paying-in-slip which would normally be used is blanked out with the words '*annulato*' meaning cancelled.

How best to make use of your bank in connection with property purchases is dealt with in the appropriate chapters.

Property purchase loans

There are a number of Italian institutions in the property mortgage market. They take the place of the UK building societies and usually they are open only to Italian nationals who are salaried and who are buying their first house. The rate of interest, subsidised by the Italian government is very low and is offered on a once only basis to encourage more people to buy their own homes. Of course there are also other credit institutions who lend to house purchasers the second or third time round but at ruinously high interest rates compared with the UK. Insurance companies do lend money but it is far from common and quite difficult to find the sort of borrowing and/or insurance policy you want particularly at the price you have in mind.

Virtually all the banks are also lenders for property purchases or will put you in touch with a subsidiary of their own which deals with home loans. Each institution has its own rules of thumb but in general terms, it should be possible to borrow up to about 75% or perhaps a little more for a permanent home and 50–60% for a holiday home. This will not be on the price you paid for the property but on the price which appears, or will appear in the conveyance to you. The length of loans in Italy is somewhat shorter than in the UK and on average ten to 15 years would be considered normal. An offer of a loan can usually be obtained quite quickly. If you are buying with the aid of a loan, it is a good idea to tie this up before signing any contract even with a proviso for the obtaining of a loan in it. Incredible as it may seem, not every lending institution demands that you insure the property — never assume that the lender has insured the property on your behalf; he almost certainly has not!

In quite a number of cases, where the loan is less than a certain amount or a certain percentage of value, the lender will not even have a valuation made and when an inspection is made of property offered for mortgage it is generally for valuation rather than for survey purposes. You will not therefore be able to find out if there are any defects in the property such as you can in the UK when, for example, a building society says that it will make a retention of part of a loan until certain repairs have been carried out.

The high rate of interest is one important reason for not having an Italian loan on a house, another is that the loan offer may forbid early repayment of part of a loan by instalments of less than ten per cent of the original loan. A penalty may be (and usually is) charged for early repayment but the government has laid down strict rules as to how much these may be. Even the sale of the house before the mortgage period is up may incur a penalty.

If a borrower defaults the lender can, of course, sell the property. If this is due to becoming unemployed or serious illness then arrangements can and almost certainly will be made to extend the period of the loan. However, even in Italy, an insurance policy can be taken out against such misfortune and what is more the premiums are allowable against income tax.

With more and more UK institutions lending money against property abroad it should not be difficult to find a mortgage which is better and cheaper than what is on offer in Italy.

11 The Italian tax system

Whether you are leaving the UK for good or whether you intend to go on living there but have only a holiday home in Italy, you must get advice from experts who know about **both** Italian and UK tax law. You should also disabuse yourself of the idea that the Italian tax system is not sophisticated and cannot catch up with you. Virtually everything is on computer now and you can be caught for as much as **seven** years back tax. They can even sell your house if necessary. Do remember that the Italians require you to make a tax declaration in keeping with your lifestyle. Thus you cannot live in a Tuscan *castello* and file a return for ten million lire a year.

For many years the Double Tax Treaty with Italy has included an arrangement for the exchange between the two countries of tax information about people. There does not seem to be so close a link between Italy and the UK as there most certainly is between Italy and certain other countries but the EC arrangements are intended to break down this reluctance.

The Italian tax system is designed to deal with taxpayers whose attitude to tax is traditionally quite different from that of the British. Quite apart from the difference in law, there is a difference in how each country views 'schemes'. Italy is still not particularly internationally minded but has a special attitude to Switzerland which is disadvantageously treated as a wicked tax haven. If you are a Swiss national, however, you will not be looked at askance for having a bank account in your home country.

Never choose a scheme which reduces you to the tortured life of a tax exile or one which costs more to operate than the tax it saves.

The following are the taxes you will come up against in Italy as a buyer (or seller) and owner of a house or flat, usually irrespective of whether you live permanently in Italy or not:

- Stamp duties payable on the purchase of property.
- VAT (IVA) on the purchase or sale of newly built houses and flats.
- VAT on food, consumer goods etc.
- Annual local taxes on the ownership of land, houses and flats (ILOR).
- Capital gains tax (INVIM) on the sale of property.
- Inheritance tax.

Resident or non-resident?

You can, of course, be resident for tax purposes in more than one country but what makes you liable to pay Italian income tax, ie makes you an Italian tax resident, is if:

- You have your home in Italy. This can be where your family live even if you spend most of your time travelling elsewhere.
- Your principal place of residence is Italy, which it is deemed to be if you spend a total of more than 183 days in any one year in that country.
- You carry on a profession or business activity in Italy unless it is ancillary to a main activity carried on elsewhere.
- The centre of your economic interests is in Italy, ie most of your investments are there or you direct your business activities which are not in Italy from that country.

Do not worry over much that the Italian tax year starts on

1 January and the UK tax year on 5 April. This can cause problems if your UK income is large enough and you are liable to Italian tax but it is one of the things which can usually be sorted out if you take advice from your accountant in good time.

Domiciled or not-domiciled?

This is a very important question. It mainly affects inheritance tax both in Italy and in the UK and also what is going to happen to what you own when you die. The answer can also decide if it is useful to make certain kinds of investments. Your domicile is the place where at any moment you intend living for the rest of your life. Husbands and wives under English law can have separate domiciles. As a very general rule, the British Inland Revenue will fight hard to claim that you have a British domicile if it will bring in inheritance tax. It helps them to prove this if you are living abroad but give any sign that Britain is still your home by saying, for example, in your Will that you would like to be buried in the plot you have bought somewhere in Britain. Advertising your domicile is so important that if you really leave Britain never to return and avow always to live in Italy, you must continue to make this clear at every possible opportunity.

Varieties of tax

Stamp duties

The current rate of stamp duty on land is 17% and on houses and flats is ten per cent. But in the case of houses and some flats in their own grounds these will be charged at ten per cent and any surplus (governed by local density regulations) will be charged at 17%. As this tax is based on the knowledge that the Italians will only declare a third of the value, the actual tax collected is just under six per cent and just over three per cent respectively. However, as a foreigner you need to be careful, as this kind of avoidance can cause you to meet a much larger capital gains tax bill (known as INVIM), which can mean paying as much as 30%. It is obvious that it is cheaper to pay almost the full stamp duty rather than capital gains tax. Your vendor will protest since it increases his CGT bill but in Italy it is a buyers' market.

Capital gains tax — INVIM *(Imposta Comunale sull' Incremento del Valore degli Immobili)*

INVIM is applicable only to real property and is paid to the *comune* in which the property is situate. It varies from three per cent to 30% depending on the profit made on sale. Over 200% profit involves a tax of 30%. Every property owner is subject to INVIM on sale with **no** exceptions. Although your INVIM bill is assessed on sale and has to be paid there and then the bank will block a certain amount of your money for two years in case the *comune* wish to re-assess the amount. Even though blocked your money can be on deposit earning interest.

VAT—IVA *(Imposta sul Valore Aggiunto)*

Of course, IVA will be payable on work done to build your house. It is more usual in Italy for prices or estimates to be quoted ex-IVA. The current rate of IVA for building work is 19%. IVA is charged on many things such as food, books and children's clothing which do not carry this tax in the UK. The rate is currently 19% but it can be higher or lower on some items such as food which is taxed at 9%.

Property tax—ILOR (*Imposte Locale sui Reditti*)

This is a local tax which is normally charged when you make an annual tax declaration. It is worked out as a small percentage of your total declaration and is allowable against your tax bill to the Italian state. If you are non-resident you are still liable for this tax and you will be charged a certain amount of ordinary income tax (IRPEF) on the grounds that you must have **some** money to live and maintain your house in Italy as well as a small sum for ILOR. The payment of this tax will not put you in the Italian tax system except on a very local basis and in a very small way.

It is worth pointing out here that many British people who have houses in Italy have not paid a lira in ILOR (some until last year were exonerated because their house was less than 25 years old but this facility has now been dropped) and have incurred fines of up to 200,000 lire per annum for every year not paid. This tax is between 40,000 and 400,000 lire per annum (depending on your income and the size of your house), derisory sums compared with the fines. Moreover, until all the ILOR bills have been paid the property cannot be transferred, thus ruling out a sale. Since this, a charge for removing rubbish and a water rate are the only annual property taxes payable in Italy, the British who do not bother to pay them are foolish in the extreme.

Income tax — IRPEF (*Imposte sui Reditti delle Pensone Fisiche*)

This is not a tax which you become liable to pay simply because you have bought property in Italy. Indeed, you could become liable to pay Italian income tax without owning any property in Italy at all, though this is very unlikely. The calculation of income tax in Italy is just as complicated as in the UK and the rates and reliefs change just as often. There is therefore little object in setting out what they are today for they will soon be different. It is perhaps worth bearing in mind that Italian income tax on high earnings is 53% which is rather more than in the UK.

However, there are many people resident in Italy who do not have to make a declaration of income each year. These are:

- Those who have no income at all.
- Those who receive **voluntary payments** from divorced husbands or wives, from their father, mother or other member of the family which can change from time to time or even be discontinued. The voluntary nature is the important factor.
- Those who receive war pensions, disability or invalid pensions or state pensions such as the old age pension.
- Those who have paid tax at source on dividends, bank deposit interest etc.
- Those who are employed in Italy, where tax will be deducted on a basis similar to PAYE in the UK.
- Those living on capital and capital gains (which are not yet taxable in Italy except where the sale of real property is concerned).
- Those living on the proceeds of gambling!

If you do become liable to Italian income tax, you will be wise to seek out an Italian accountant known as a *commercialistà* who will sort things out for you quickly and efficiently. As pointed out in 'Living in Italy': 'As some fines for a wrongful declaration can reach one million lire it is frankly unwise to complete your own declaration unless you are a qualified Italian accountant'. Employing a *commercialistà* is not particularly expensive when you take into account the money and tax he can save you.

Declarations must be filed and tax paid in full by 31 May every year. Once in the tax system you must pay 95% of the tax you paid the previous year by 30 November. Again if you have earned less than this it becomes the province of an accountant. Never think in terms of a rebate — the Italians can take years to pay the money back. It is better that you should pay the minimum. Requests for a rebate must be made within 18 months of the claim arising. Two years appears to be the minimum wait to receive your money back.

Inheritance tax *(Imposte di successione)*

In three respects, *imposte di successione* differs radically from its English counterpart:

- The tax is not payable out of the estate generally at a rate which is linked to the value of the assets of the person who has died.
- The rate at which the tax is paid depends on the relationship of the beneficiary to the person who has died and each beneficiary is liable for his own tax.
- There is no surviving spouse exemption.

The tax on gifts, *imposte di donazione*, is calculated in the same manner as *imposte di successione* by reference to the amount of the gift and the relationship of the maker of the gift to the receiver.

The impact of *imposte di successione*, the manner in which it is assessed and the persons on whom it falls make it essential, if you intend to acquire property of any kind in Italy, to take the most competent advice as to inheritance tax and plan your investments accordingly.

There is no tax payable on an estate of less than 30 million lire (about £13,500).

Between parents and children (both ways) the maximum tax paid on an estate is 31% and this is when the value of the estate reaches 1,000 million lire (about £450,000). At the other end of the scale a totally unrelated person, ie a friend or a charity **not** recognised by the Italian state (and **most are not**), starts paying inheritance tax from one million lire upwards. The scale goes up to 60% at the 1000 million lire stage, almost 30% more than between father and child.

Bridging loans are relatively easy to obtain from your Italian bank for the purpose of paying the duty, which must be paid in advance of the property, cash, etc being transferred to the beneficiary.

Offshore companies

For some years, the Italian tax authorities have been aware that the use of non-Italian companies as owners of land in their country can lead to the reduction of Italian tax.

The successful use of a non-Italian company for this purpose involves a considerable amount of expert knowledge and no-one should ever indulge in an exercise of this kind without specialised advice.

12 Things to bear in mind

Whatever you may buy in Italy — flat or house, new or old — there are a number of points which need special thought. Italy is a highly civilized country but not in the way you would expect. Certain things are done differently and you will be in for considerable surprises (not necessarily pleasant) if you do not take this into account from the very beginning.

Utilities

Water

Except in the northern, mountainous regions and the Po valley Italy is extremely short of water and you are liable to be cut off in the summer without any notice. Indeed it is wise to expect to be cut off — having a constant supply of water on tap in July, August and September should be counted as a bonus. If you are on city or mains water you will have little problem about pressure etc but if you are in the country (the deeper the country, the greater the problems) you will undoubtedly suffer from both water shortages and low pressure. It pays in Italy to make enquiries about this and have a tank of about 1000 litres for household purposes and, if you are a keen gardener and are allowed to do so, another tank of some 50,000 litres which will last about a month and a half in a smallish garden. Many houses in the drier parts of Italy are built with vast tanks under the house to cope with just such problems. It goes without saying that if you intend to do this you must get planning permission before beginning work.

If your supply is not mains, it is worthwhile testing it for purity from time to time or installing a filter but the occasions when this would be necessary will be rare and it is usually after very heavy rain that the water becomes muddy, rather than when there is a drought. Water stored in large holding tanks should not be used for drinking or cooking. Water passing through 1000 litre tanks via a pump, however, is fit for drinking.

You need not worry about the quality of the mains water which is regularly tested. If the water is passed as *potabile*, it is drinkable. If you are relying on your own source of water from a spring or river you will find this will be tested from time to time (at your expense!) and passed for drinking or not.

Water source

What is much more important if you are buying a country property or having a new house built for you in the country is to make absolutely sure that you have an undoubted source of water which belongs to you and cannot be turned off by your neighbour or drained away by surrounding owners. Of course if you are connected up to the water tank of the local *comune* you will not need to make any other arrangements but you will be charged an annual water rate. Much country property depends on local wells for water and it is often difficult to establish from the title deeds who owns them and who has the right to share them. You must get this absolutely clear before you buy. The odds are that you will find after you have bought the property at least one and probably more than one unauthorised user of your supply of water. Whether you maintain good neighbourly relationships by saying nothing or complain is up to you but do remember that, just as in the UK, an unauthorised use of your water, like a right of way, can become authorised after a number of years of uninterrupted use. Even the local authority is not blameless in such matters. No matter how convenient from a technical viewpoint never install a pump outside the limits of your own property because eventually the local authority may claim it as their property.

Laying of pipes

The other thing which appals non-Italians coming to live in the countryside is the very casual way the locals go about laying the water supply pipes. These are just laid on the top of the earth (they are usually made of galvanised steel but are sometimes plastic), thoroughly exposed to all the elements and in the mountainous regions it can be very cold in winter. In the Dolomites for instance they are at least put underground. The Italians are most philosophical about burst pipes particularly when one considers they are not reimbursed by insurance companies except on a third party basis. There is nothing to stop you from insulating your pipes where they exit from the local *vasco* (small local reservoir) and indeed this helps to distinguish your own pipes later on. The Germans make an excellent extruded polystyrene pipe-covering which stands up quite well to Italian winters.

The household pump

The other problem in the country is that you will almost certainly need a pump to increase the pressure of your household water. Otherwise you will find the gas water heaters will not function properly and it will take a long time to run any amount of water. This is known as an *autoclave* in Italian and should always be put under cover since wet weather can inhibit its proper functioning. In general the installation of an *autoclave* and 2 × 500 litre tanks (again undercover since they are not items of great beauty) should cost in the region of two to three million lire.

Electricity

The voltage in Italy is 230 with the usual tolerance and is AC. Because of installation costs etc, there are places in the country where people generate their own, either AC or DC though usually the former since it is now simple to buy a

Japanese generator (preferably **out** of Italy) which supplies AC current.

Electrical installation

Wiring is supposed to be in accordance with EC rules but frequently is not, particularly in old houses, although the green/yellow earth wire is fairly universal. Otherwise ENEL, the nationalised electricity board, is the sole supplier and normally will provide a supply even in the depths of the country (although this could perhaps be expensive if you are the only consumer in the area — think in terms of three to five million lire for bringing electricity to you in the back of beyond). If you are building in an area where ENEL already supply other houses the charges will be about one tenth of that. When building you will need site electricity and that can be very expensive indeed — around 120,000 lire per month so the quicker you get on to a normal supply the better for you.

When you install electricity for the first time in a new property which you yourself have built or had built for you, ENEL will come and inspect the installation, checking the wiring, its gauge and how many earth trips there are. Until your house has passed that test they will not link you up to the supply. By and large Italian electrical installations are of high quality and extremely safe since earth trips (circuit breakers) are frequently used; for instance, every washing machine, dishwasher, oven, bathroom light has to have its own circuit breaker installed, often known as a *differenziale.* You will find these are quite expensive bits of equipment. Most people find them **too** sensitive and certainly as far as electric lawn mowers are concerned the Italian *differenziale* works quicker than the special cut-out available from lawn mower suppliers.

Change of ownership

On a change of ownership, ENEL may check the wiring if it is an old house but frequently they do not. Having changed house, flat or been cut off for non-payment do not expect

ENEL to rush to reconnect you — they take their time (ten days can be fairly standard) and often it requires your presence in person at their offices to get anything done.

Bills

Electricity bills are rendered every two months and are always estimated except for those in December and June when you are presented with a *conguaglio* or 'settling-up' and this can come as something of a shock.

If you are not always in Italy it is best to pay your electricity, gas and telephone bills by direct debit from your bank account in Italy, making sure you have allowed enough for the *conguaglio* and for bank charges which often the bank does not tell you about until two months after they have taken the money.

Of course if you live in Italy it is not difficult to pay these bills by cheque or at the post office.

The worst news comes last. The most electricity ENEL will supply is 3 kw per contract. If you wish for more you must have a separate contract with a separate standing charge. Electricity is expensive when compared with the UK or neighbouring France or Switzerland and ENEL's employees, in the country certainly, have no compunction in turning it off for their convenience without so much as a whisper of warning. Therefore those buying fax machines should ensure they have a battery which will take over for up to a couple of hours and those using word processors should 'save' every ten minutes or so.

Gas

Except in towns, you must expect not to have mains gas. Where you do, you will find the system is very similar to that for electricity — you will only be given a supply if your own piping is in order and you will be charged in the same way as for electricity. All non-Italian appliances must be tested (at your expense) and found to conform to Italian standards.

Bottled gas

Where you do not have a supply of town gas (and this includes not only villages and deep country but also houses and flats in towns where the builders have not provided gas) you must rely on bottled gas and this is a common practice. Many people who prefer to cook with gas will have gas stoves with small bottles of gas under the sink or on the balcony. This will affect your insurance premium. In the case of country properties, if you are only using gas to cook, a bottle of gas will suffice and will last for an average family for about six weeks. Remember to always have a spare bottle. The method is fairly wasteful as one never manages fully to exhaust a bottle.

Do not be afraid to use bottled gas since it is quite safe if you observe the rules. If your hot water system and/or central heating system is also by gas, you will need a gas tank or you will spend your life changing bottles. These tanks are subject to very strict safety regulations and can only be sited in certain places on a property. This is best left to the suppliers of your gas to deal with. In many cases, you will get a free installation in exchange for using a chosen supplier's gas. This sort of gas tank is known as a *bombolone* and is never allowed to be put underground. You will need to have a cement platform built to accommodate the gas tank. It must be surrounded by a wire fence approximately two metres high, have a locked door (you keep one key and give the other to the gas company) and have a fire extinguisher (however, in the event of fire it is not recommended that you go and fight it anywhere near a gas tank). This is the most expensive way of central heating though very efficient. Central heating with town gas, on the other hand is probably the cheapest method.

Oil

This is the next cheapest form of central heating. If you can face the thought of paying for the transport of an oil-fired Aga from the UK this is probably the least expensive form of heating and is much to be recommended in Italian alpine regions, the Veneto, Friuli and the mountains north of Milan. Over the years the cost of transport will be amortised. Do not be side-tracked into a Rayburn or Italian oil-fired stove — they all lose heat and are not so efficient or economical.

Telephone

The telephone system in Italy is principally run by an organisation called SIP (*Società Italiana per l'Esercizio delle Telecomunicazioni, p.a.*) although Italcable deal with overseas calls (you get their bill on your ordinary SIP bill months later) and one or two other companies are involved as well. Over the years SIP have managed to get parliament to pass various stringent laws, the net result of which is that they have virtually a monopoly on telecommunications in Italy. For instance you cannot have a cordless telephone, a bleeper or pager, computers which plug into the telephone network etc, without getting them from SIP and they never go in for special offers. Any other sort of telephone, extension etc, must have been passed by SIP though this is more honoured in the breach than in the observance. When you sign a contract with SIP you get one telephone on rental and all extensions have to be purchased at around 200,000 lire a time, for an instrument you can buy in the shops for approximately one third of that price. So far as cordless telephones are concerned the situation is rather more serious. First of all SIP say quite rightly that many of the cordless telephones made in Korea or Taiwan are dangerous (they actually attract lightning — a common occurrence in Italy) and in certain circumstances can kill a person. That said, what they have to offer is cumbersome, indeed hardly portable, has a limited range and costs 1.7 million lire as opposed to around 200–250,000 lire. If a SIP employee sees a cordless telephone not from SIP he is bound to report it. The fine is 600–750,000 lire and the telephone can be confiscated. So be very circumspect.

Fax machines

Although SIP sell fax machines under their own name (they are Panasonic) there are no bargains compared to the prices in the shops. Moreover every telefax machine must have been passed by the Italian Standards Institute (ie SIP in this case) and every machine has a tax imposed on it of some 35,000 lire every two months. Failure to pay this tax to the government (it goes on your SIP bill) is an offence. With foreign machines it is difficult to get them serviced in Italy. SIP frequently test lines for cordless telephones, faxes etc.

Hire purchase

Always be cautious of entering into a hire purchase agreement with SIP. It is far cheaper to buy whatever machine you want on a credit card and pay it off as you wish without paying invoices for setting up the dossier etc, and being forced to have a maintenance agreement at 120,000 lire every two months. Anyone entering into a hire purchase agreement feels it is usually a painless way, in spite of the interest element. However, the SIP leasing department is notoriously slow and it can take anything up to a year from the date you signed all the forms until your bank gets their first demand for payment. All well and good if it were for one payment only but in fact it is for all the payments due until that date. Thus a fax machine that you can obtain in commerce for around three million lire costs five million lire via SIP. Leasing you can find yourself paying out as much as two million lire at one go. This sum may well include interest payments for late payment. Generally it is best to avoid hire purchase agreements altogether.

Installation

There is not usually much delay in obtaining a telephone except possibly in very remote areas. Usually this has to be done by a visit to your local SIP office armed with your passport and, if you can obtain it, a Residence Certificate from your local town hall which will allow you to have the cheaper rental. As soon as a line is available, you will get a letter confirming the number you have been given. If there is a waiting list for phones and you need one as a matter of urgency — if you are an invalid or for some other good reason — a doctor's letter or similar support will give you priority. Of course, if you live in a very inaccessible spot you may well find there is some time to wait for a telephone and when it does come you will have a large bill to pay for its installation. The maximum charge is set by statute but when you see it or are told of it that will be of little comfort. It is usually around 200,000 lire for a new installation and half that sum for a transfer. In town it is relatively inexpensive to have a telephone connected but in some large cities there is a tremendous waiting list.

Bills

Bills come every two months and can be paid by direct debit from your bank or by cash at a post office or SIP office or by cheque to your local area office. If you think that it is unlikely that you will have been overcharged, it is best to pay by direct debit. If you want a receipt for the payment, you must pay in cash and if you fear that the payment will get lost, you must pay at the local area office.

Tariffs

Calls in Italy cost on average 30% more than in the UK and that is ordinary tariff. If you telephone between 8.30 am and 1.30 pm you pay a 40% surcharge on all calls whether they are local, STD or overseas. That means to chat to a friend in London mid-morning on Wednesday will cost you 70% more than if you were ringing from the UK. Ordinary tariff is from 1.30 to 6.30 pm then comes evening tariff from 6.30 to 10 pm and from then on until 8 am the next morning the charges are greatly reduced. In the morning you can get ordinary tariff between 8 and 8.30 am. Ordinary tariff also prevails until 1.00 pm on Saturday and thereafter you get the evening rate until 10 pm. The evening rate applies until 10 pm on all public holidays. Be warned that calls to some countries are never allowed at anything but the full rate — the Persian Gulf for instance. Calls made via the operator, as in most countries, cost more.

Services

So for all this expense what do you get? A very polite and helpful service. Sometimes the foreign (and Italian) directories are not very up to date but, although you pay for directory enquiries made abroad, the operators will take any amount of trouble and in the international section usually speak the language of the country concerned.

There are most of the usual services offered such as alarm calls, weather forecasts, snow forecasts, speaking clock — but in Italian of course — regional recipes, stock exchange news, horoscopes, etc, etc.

Public telephone boxes are all going over to cards or cards and *gettoni* (telephone tokens) the latter of which cost 200 lire each and give you very little time. As in many countries it is quite difficult to find a box which takes money. In northern and central Italy telephone boxes are rarely vandalised and SIP keep them clean but there are not nearly enough of them. The international telephone card exists in Italy but at the moment only at SIP offices. Reversed charges or collect calls still exist but it should be remembered that you, the payer of the call, also get charged 1,500 lire each time, to add insult to injury.

Emergency calls from boxes need a coin, card or *gettone* — the coin or *gettone* will be returned and the number to ring is 113 for fire, police or ambulance. However, everyone who has lived in Italy will tell you that having rung the Fire Service or for an Ambulance it is always a good idea to ring the Carabinieri on 112 and tell them what you have done and they will follow it up and get things moving. Of course you cannot do this if you have called for the local police since the two cannot check up on each other.

If you have a telephone out of order you ring 183 where you will get a recorded message telling you to dial **your own number**. You will hear no ringing tone but will be answered — eventually.

12 is the number to ring for ordinary directory enquiries.

15 will get you the operator, if you want to make an international call via the operator, or if you want directory enquiries you dial 15 followed by the code for the country concerned. Thus 15–44 for a British number.

Telegrams can still be dictated over Italian telephones — and in English but you will have to make your request first in Italian. The number to dial is 186. Bear in mind though that not all countries still have a cable or telegram service. International collect or reversed charge calls still exist in Italy but in many European countries this service has been abolished. The operator will tell you if a country has or has not a system for reverse charge calls.

Television

Italy uses the same television system as the British and therefore you can bring your television set to Italy if you wish. This must be declared at the frontier **at the same time as bringing your furniture or belongings** in and your name, address will be taken in order to send you a reminder when the next licence is due. You pay for three, six, nine months or a year at the moment of entering Italy. Alternatively, if there is no-one to perform this task, which is quite likely, you purchase a licence at your local post office. Do not think you can get away without a licence since there are detector vans all over the country and the Italian fines for not having a licence are enormous when compared with the UK equivalent.

Dish aerials to receive television programmes from various satellites are quite common in Italy but in order to get BBC programmes you should write to the BBC Technical Department stating accurately where you live and giving longitude and latitude and stating whether there are mountains nearby. They in turn will give you directions as to how to place your dish for the best reception.

If you want to get French programmes you will need to have a dual standard set, ie SECAM and PAL — the same goes for using French video cassettes.

You will almost certainly want to receive something else as well as Italian television. However, it is quite a good way of improving your Italian particularly if you live in places where the local accent is difficult to understand such as Venice and the Veneto, Bergamo or Liguria.

Sewage

If you live in a city, town or even a small village, drainage and sewage problems will not concern you and you will also have a bill for clearing away your rubbish and refuse.

Septic tanks

However, if you are in the country, it is very probable that your house or block of flats will be connected not to main drainage but to a septic tank. Rules about these differ very much from those in the UK and their construction is strictly regulated. If you have a private septic tank of your own, make certain that you know how often it needs emptying and where you go to to have this done. Encourage your guests to be circumspect about what they try to dispatch towards the tank. Do not forget that normal emptying of a septic tank is one thing but unblocking it is quite another and far less pleasant job. If you are building your own house, make certain, among other things, that the septic tank is placed where it can easily be reached and you know exactly where it is. Never install the minimum septic tank allowed for your property. It is better to err on the generous side. Having one which is **double** the minimum required is quite a good idea and what you pay extra on installation you save on pumping out operations over the years.

When you have a swimming pool in Italy, for which you **always** need planning permission, you will also need a separate septic tank. It is useless to explain that you never change the water from one year to the next, you will be forced to have a very large and very expensive septic tank and this should be taken into account when costing a swimming pool.

Running costs and maintenance

Do not forget when considering the cost of property in Italy that once you have paid the price, you will be involved in annual running costs.

- There are standing charges for electricity, gas, telephone and the like which have to be paid whether or not you are using the property.
- There are local taxes for rubbish collection and water to be paid if you are a tenant and you pay both these and a property tax if you are both owner and occupier.
- If you live in a condominium you will have service charges to pay.
- There will be insurance premiums on both your property and its contents.

At the time you are thinking of buying, it should be possible to assess the total of all these liabilities. To foresee what they will be in a few years time is far more difficult. Remember that a seller of property or his agent is liable to quote you figures for outgoings at the lower end of the scale and if you cannot get independent advice on this, add on at least 20% to the figures you are given for safety.

Whilst the cost of maintaining your block and its surroundings, if you live in a flat, will be included in your service charge, you will want to maintain the interior. If you live in a house, both exterior and interior are your direct concern. Remember that Italy is a long country and one with wide property price variations. It follows that the need, for example, to paint externally is as frequent in the north as in England but much less frequent in the south. Where property is expensive, workmen are expensive so that all in all, you must expect considerable price variations when it comes to maintenance. All that can be said with any degree of certainty is that the further south you go, the less swiftly will your workmen arrive to do the job but that is part of the southern way of life.

Insurance

Until relatively recently it was against the law to insure an asset situate in Italy with a non-Italian company. This was for exchange control reasons, to prevent Italians receiving the payment of claims made outside Italy which they failed to repatriate and to prevent them hiding their assets from the Italian Inland Revenue. It is still against the law to take out the obligatory third party, fire and theft cover for an Italian registered car other than with a company with offices in Italy.

Only during the last 15 or 20 years have Italians started to insure their property and there are still parts of the peninsula where less than ten per cent of the houses are insured. However, where forest fires are likely many, many more houses will be insured. No Italian company will give earthquake cover since the argument is that the government will pay. At a slightly higher premium you can usually get earthquake cover at Lloyds.

You are now allowed to insure with Lloyds in London through a Lloyds broker (one who is prepared to insure an Italian asset, since not all are) provided the policy carries a tax (payable by you) which is the equivalent of the VAT you would pay on an Italian Policy and provided this is paid to the Italian State by Lloyds and the policy is registered.

Italian insurance policies

There are many reasons why you should avoid using Italian policies if you can. The first and most important is that there are far too many things they will not pay for, from burst pipes due to freezing weather to the loss of jewellery unless it is in the safe. The second is that it is virtually impossible to cancel insurance policies which run from one year (very unusual) to ten years (the most common). These latter are always thrust on newcomers and later as your Italian improves and you complain, you will be told that everyone knows that household policies run for ten years. Policies are most unclear. For instance, unless you are very careful, you can find yourself paying for a ski-holiday insurance which only gets you off the mountain, repatriates you to Italy then only pays for the difference between the National Health Scheme and a limited amount of private consultation. Unless you can read rather complicated insurance Italian you probably thought you were buying something quite different.

In addition, where contents and jewellery are concerned, there are valuation difficulties if any of the items have been bought in the UK. Italian and English values differ considerably. For example, what is considered to be average quality carpet in England would be so expensive in Italy as to be almost unknown so that no-one will believe the value you give it. Jewellery on the other hand is much cheaper in Italy though many English and French jewellers think that the gems they use are not of top quality. Also anything less than

18 carat gold is not counted as gold in spite of the fortune you paid. Watches more than three years old have little value even if they are Patek Philippe.

Jewellery and household silver must be kept in a locked safe except when in use and the safe must be accompanied by a certificate to the insurance company that it was fitted by a qualified person. The Italian insurance company will give you a list of safes you can use — otherwise nothing is covered. If you are mugged, lose your engagement ring at a nightclub, lose a stone out of a pair of earrings, you are not covered. Books are covered at only 1,000 lire each on some policies — this in a country where the average Italian book costs 20,000 lire and the average English book 25–30,000 lire minimum.

A Lloyds policy

Therefore, everything points to having a Lloyds policy. You will need a local valuation done by a *geometrà* for your house and to produce bills for the contents unless they are antiques which means they were probably previously insured in the UK. You will need proper mortise locks on all entry doors, locks on the shutters and if you are away for more than a certain period each year, ie it is a holiday home, then you will pay an extra premium — but so you would in the UK. If you have valuables then Lloyds will almost certainly demand you have a safe. But when you have an all risks policy it will be just that and you will be covered if you lose something away from home.

Crime

For all its reputation Italy is not the criminal sink of iniquity it is said to be. Certainly burglaries and thefts of all sorts are common in the large cities, particularly places like Milan, Florence and tourist resorts. The insurance companies are well aware of the burglary figures and will insist on proper locks and usually on a safe. However, in the country life is generally peaceful and burglaries are quite rare. This is partly due to the fact that the Italians believe that if you had real money you would not bother living in the back of beyond but would be living in central Milan or Venice. The tradition of the elegant country house is not quite so entrenched in Italy as it is in Britain.

Nevertheless, you would be wise to have proper locks, well fitting shutters and perhaps a safe if you have anything worth stealing.

In virtually every town, big or small there is a drug problem — in the large cities it is a major problem and therefore, unless you are very careful and have an alarm (or even just a sticky label saying you have one) on your car it will sooner or later be broken into. This is a fact of urban life today. Always use a radio or tape-recorder in your car which can be removed and locked into the boot or under the front seat. It also should not look as though you have done just that, leaving a gaping hole announcing to all and sundry that somewhere in the car is something worth stealing.

There is no point in having a burglar-alarm which rings for the police — they simply do not answer. A better bet is to make sure front and back doors have proper locks and hinge bolts, that all the windows lock and that all the shutters lock also — anodised aluminium shutters with mild-steel bars in the middle are better than the prettier wooden ones though there are parts of old towns and villages where these are not allowed for artistic reasons. Many Italians use grilles known as *cancelli* and these are very difficult to get past. Do not, though, make your home such a fortress that you cannot get out in a hurry if need be.

13 Letting your property

The Rent Act

Income tax is not the main problem for once in this case. The real problem is that there is a very restrictive rent act in Italy and once one enters that net one is caught for years with a tenant at a low, usually uneconomic rent. This applies particularly in large cities.

It is highly unlikely you will be lucky enough to find property for rent under this scheme which favours tenants and which is known as *equo canone*. If you can then jump at it.

The moment you register a lease for letting it is made subject to *equo canone* thus all leases that anyone sensible has are without benefit of the law. The disadvantage of this is if the tenant does not pay his rent or damages the property you cannot, under Italian law go to court and sue him.

Letting choices

Holiday rentals, ie for less than three months at a time, are not subject to *equo canone* and you are at liberty to make your own arrangements without breaking the law. If you let your property for longer periods you will, strictly speaking, be breaking the law.

As in Britain, where similar rules apply, never, never let a property that is not at least basically furnished. The rules are rather more flexible with furnished property.

Letting to a company or corporate body is not quite so attractive as it is in Britain but you would be wise to register the lease which means, of course, you pay tax on the income.

Tenants

The best way to find holiday tenants is through British agents, villa agents, the Sunday newspapers and if possible visit future tenants **in their own homes** to see how they live. Always take at least a 50% deposit by way of deposit which can later be used as a deposit against breakages. Then nearer the time of occupation ask for the full rental, ie 100%, keeping the first 50% for breakages. Once you have found the property in proper condition after departure the 50% breakages deposit should be returned. Italian telephones are expensive and if your tenants want to have one they should pay extra. Beware tenants who say they do not want a telephone and then arrive with their own cordless one and plug it into your socket. If they do not want it you should have it disconnected.

Try not to let your property through Italian estate agents, not because they are dishonest, but because you may well get little Italian children messing-up your house or flat. Also it is impossible to vet anyone unless you are on the spot and even then Italians can be so charming and eminently presentable that you cannot believe they would ever harm your possessions. Alas, Italians have little civic sense and whilst they may be spotless in their own home, and usually are, on holiday the attitude becomes 'I've paid for it and they can clear up afterwards'.

There are several British people making a very good living out of letting, cleaning and generally running furnished property and provided you have a reference from someone else this can be an excellent method of finding the right sort of tenant. Most of them are around Tuscany, Umbria or the northern lakes. They will undertake collecting the rents and deposits and so on and will charge you a percentage. Make sure you are given a complete list of their charges before committing yourself.

Tax implications

If you are resident in the UK for tax purposes you should of course declare this income. If you are resident in Italy for tax purposes you should declare it to the Italian Revenue. Few Italians do. They ask the tenants to say to any visiting *Guardia di Finanza* (Customs & Excise) employee that they are a cousin, brother in law, close friend, etc, of the owner and to point out that they are not paying rent.

The tax due depends on your overall annual income — in Italy there is no difference between earned and unearned income — and only by November of each year will you discover how much is expected of you. If you make a practice of letting your property and declaring it you will be allowed certain sums for repairs etc, to be set against the tax chargeable.

You should always inform your insurance company when you are letting your property since the risks are somewhat altered.

14 Extending your property

First of all it is not a good idea to build what you feel is a basic house to which you will add on parts later. This is because you may well wait ten years before you are allowed to add any more living space and then at that date only some ten per cent extra may be allowed. You should include the space in the house you are building so that you will be able to finish these parts later on. You may well get planning permission for a 130 square metre house and decide to only build 100 square metres. In theory this is a good idea — you could use the other 30 square metres later on for a large bedroom and bathroom. In practice alas, it does not work since your planning permission for 130 square metres will not last for ever and you may find that a couple of years after the completion you will not get planning permission to extend. Moreover, you will have the extra cost of a *collaudo* as if it were a whole house, the extra cost of planning permission, to say nothing of the architect's or *geometrà*'s fees which will be proportionately higher than for a whole house. The journeys undertaken by these people and the period of time they spend on the project are almost as long as if you were building an entire house. It is not just the expense of the undertaking that makes this a plan not to be recommended but also the uncertainty of Italian planning permission and the long intervals between the changing of the density regulations.

However, there frequently occurs in Italy the sudden knowledge that the density regulations have been increased in an area — it is done zone by zone for each *comune*. If there are builders on the Building Committee of the local *comune* (*Commissione Edilizia*) it has been found that the extension percentages granted are much more generous — often as much as 30%. This, on the average property of 100 to 120 square metres, will provide another bedroom and bathroom or even two small bedrooms. At this point it is worth considering an extension.

Planning permission

Extending your property can cover many things and you will need planning permission for them all, irrespective of whether they increase the living area or not. The range of extensions can vary from a covered terrace in your garden, a swimming pool (which will need it's own septic tank and space for housing the machinery) to a car-port. You do not need planning permission for small greenhouses or garden sheds.

External changes

By and large you can plant what you wish in your garden in the way of trees and shrubs but you cannot remove trees (even those you have planted) unless they are dead. It is best to take a photograph of the dead tree before rooting it up. Hedges must not be within 1.5 metres of your neighbour's land and should not put his in shadow. He could complain but it is most unlikely that he will do so officially.

However, if you live in a well known beauty spot or on a *strada panoramica*, a scenic route, you must not build or plant anything that will block the view of the public. This **can** affect your privacy and the only way to get round it is to build a hedge around the terrace where you sit out and eat. Alternatively, you can plant a small tree which will become very large over the years. Trees are sacred in Italy and will never be removed unless they are dangerous, so people will be asked to move to one or other side of it to enjoy the view.

You will need planning permission to build walls and terraces in your garden, but if there was a wall, for example, that at one stage existed on your property but was demolished, you will be allowed to replace it without any lengthy procedures. Most repair work is not chargeable for planning permission. However, if you are going to re-landscape your garden and terraces you will need to submit plans and almost certainly you will be required to build such walls and terrace in reinforced concrete with stone facing. If a terrace falls down, or you have a landslide, *frana* in Italian, take a photograph and include it with your request for planning permission.

Even though such works are relatively minor you must not commence them until you have the licence *(licenza)* in your hand.

Changes to the house

When you are building extensions to a house or changing the use of rooms or spaces, ie a utility room or garage into a guest bedroom you need to employ an architect or *geometrà* and gain planning permission. For anything that increases the living area of the house, you will need planning permission. However, it is also possible to increase the living area of your house without actually adding an extension. The most important thing to remember is that the ceiling heights are important — a garage or utility room which has only a 2.5 metre ceiling height will never be allowed to be used for living space. However if it is possible to convert then remember that you will need permission for the car-port you are probably going to have instead.

A most important thing to remember is that you cannot, necessarily, do all your extensions on the ground floor only. If the house is a two storey house you may well have to divide the extra space equally between the ground floor and first floor. This you must get your architect to thrash out with the *comune*.

Changes to the interior

You are free to do more or less anything to the interior except pull down load bearing walls or close up a small kitchen which is open plan (probably because it is too small to be anything other than open plan). A kitchen should have a minimum area of nine or ten square metres before it is allowed to have a door which closes it off from the rest of the house. Hence the popularity of open plan kitchens in new blocks of flats. You must never change the exterior or the building line without permission of the *comune*. However, there is nothing to stop you putting up **wooden** pergolas or climbing plants on the house.

Tax implications

Conversions count as new building work so you will have to pay IVA (VAT) on the building works and it will then be registered on your land registry plan. You will also pay marginally more ILOR (local *comune* taxes) per annum than before. All your contracts, bills etc should be carefully kept to set against your INVIM (capital gains tax) bill when you sell the property or for when it is valued on your death.

Apartments

For those living in apartments the rules are rather stricter. The most commonly wanted work is to glass in the balcony. This is rarely allowed by the administrator of the block for obvious reasons. If everyone managed their own conversions the character of the block would change, probably for the worse, and the values would plummet accordingly. You also need special permission to put up a parabolic dish aerial on the roof and you need permission to knock down interior walls etc (you will never get permission to knock down a load bearing wall).

15 Settling in

You have bought your property and chosen it to fit in best with your future intentions. It may be just a holiday home or it may be that you have decided to live in Italy on a permanent basis or it may be that what is now only for holidays will become your home on retirement. As you will have seen from chapter 10 on the Italian tax system, it is very unlikely in practice that you will become liable to Italian income tax unless you have your permanent home there. On the other hand, it is fairly safe to assume that if you obtain the necessary permission to reside permanently in Italy you will fall into the Italian tax net. Few people need give much more thought to the technical difference between residence for tax purposes and residence for other purposes.

Applying for permanent residence

You are a citizen of an EC country and this of itself gives you certain rights to reside and to work in every other EC country. This freedom is not quite unlimited because most countries like to keep a check on foreigners. To reside on **any** basis in Italy, you need formal permission to do so. As a British citizen, you may stay in the country for three months at a time without any formalities except filling in a *Dichiarazione di Soggiorno per Stranieri* or Foreigners' Declaration of Stay. In the first instance this is done at the local offices of the *comune* in which you are staying and such a declaration lasts three months. You supply three photographs and a great deal of information (including for instance your and your mother's maiden name). Thereafter, if you intend to stay on in Italy you renew this at either the offices of the state police (*Polizia di Stato*) or if you live in the country with the local *carabinieri*. You cannot launch into a year's stay until you have had returned the declaration for the first three months. Thereafter, your *soggiorno*, as it is known throughout Italy, will be renewed every five years at your request. However, you may well wait for three or four months before you get the form back from the local provincial offices of the Ministry of the Interior. On a straw poll it seems that the *carabinieri* ask you less questions and return your form rather more quickly than the state police in a large town.

What sort of questions do they ask?

Basically, the two things that worry any host country are whether the person they are allowing to reside in their country will become a charge on the state or whether he will need hospital treatment. Therefore, you will be asked whether you intend to reside permanently in Italy (some people with holiday homes take out a *soggiorno* each year for the sake of convenience because it does not necessarily make you resident) and if so what you are going to live on. They will ask you if you are an old age state pensioner which will automatically entitle you to free medical attention and hospitalisation (after a certain amount of form filling and exchanging), whether you have employment or are self-employed and if neither of these two things apply whether you will have remittances from your home country. They prefer to see a Form E 111 issued by the British DSS in Newcastle or some evidence of private health insurance. It is a little more complicated if you are going to work and then a work permit will be sought by your employer. (NB, it is not **your** job to do this and do not let any Italian employer tell you otherwise.) Such a permit will automatically put you into the Italian social security and tax system and being in the Italian system will answer a lot of the questions the police may put to you. For an ordinary non-employed or retired person such an interview with the police does not put you into the Italian tax system as it would in many countries. The Italians are interested only in keeping an eye on the foreign population in their country, which with terrorists like the Red Brigade existing is hardly surprising.

In answer to their questions, do not pitch your income so low that they wonder how you can live honestly. You will not be asked to produce evidence of income or means of subsistence nor will you be escorted to the frontier if you fall on hard times. The only circumstance in which you will be asked, or forced to leave is if you have been involved, or are suspected of having been involved, in criminal activity.

Italian Identity Cards are not obligatory (an Italian without one would be highly suspect) and you are not required to carry identification on you, except your driving licence when driving a car or motorbike.

As in all cases in Italy when any kind of identity document is needed, you must arm yourself with at least three passport size photographs and remember that the *carta bollata* (usually at 5000 lire) with which you pay for the document you want, is obtainable only at some tobacconists, by no means all, and never at the Post Office or the local municipal offices.

Driving licences

The moment you become resident in Italy you must exchange your English driving licence and get an Italian one in exchange. You must also re-register your car if it has English plates. Normally you will be given back your UK licence once all the details have been taken but bear in mind that the Italians do check with Swansea.

There are curious rules in Italy about who may and who may not drive certain cars. Basically if you are a foreign national but an Italian resident you should have changed your English plates for Italian ones. This involves having your car tested at the local provincial testing station for brakes, transmission, lighting (which will have had the beam changed for Italy) etc. Except with a hired car you may **NOT** drive any car in Italy which does not have Italian plates — and strictly speaking no foreigner should drive your Italian registered car though this is less important, particularly when you have given written permission. Therefore without this, you cannot drive your mother's, sister's or your friend's car and if you are caught doing so you run the risk of having the car confiscated by the police. One way round this problem is to keep your British driving licence with you when driving a foreign car (never do this in your own area where you are known) which will have a British address on it. Unless you admit you are an Italian resident no policeman or *carabiniere* is going to suspect you are. But you must have no evidence of being an Italian resident (such as an Italian driving licence or Italian identity card) on you.

Italian law requires that the car's papers (ie the Italian log book) and your Italian driving licence are carried **with you in the car at all times**. There is no question of going to a police station within three or five days with them. Your car can be sequestered if you cannot produce your papers. You are required to display the road tax disc and the insurance receipt on the windscreen of your car and insurance companies give you a special stick-on holder for this purpose. You have a fortnight's grace both for the road tax licence (known as a *bollo*) and for the insurance providing you are driving in Italy. The green card you will automatically get with your insurance policy expires on the date shown on the document and you are not covered abroad. Also if you wish to lend your car to someone who is going to drive it out of Italy you must go to an Italian notary and make such a declaration. There is a small fee for this. If you do not do this the car is **not** insured except on a third party basis only and then there will be problems.

Perhaps one should mention here that there are thousands of British people who on the one hand wish to take advantage of being resident in Italy but who still run their cars with British plates (but not paying the British road tax disc) and on English insurance. This is not only illegal but it is immoral and they would be the first to complain if every Italian working in England tried to do the same thing to avoid paying for a road tax disc. The Italian police are beginning to crack down on this. The anonymity of the cities makes it difficult for them to check easily but in the country towns and countryside the *carabinieri* are often very efficient in their mopping-up operations. Remember, in the country you go to the *carabinieri* for your *soggiorno* or residence permission. They know if you are resident all year round or not. If you are resident and are seen driving a foreign car you may well be picked up. If you are lucky you will get a warning — if you are unlucky the car will be impounded and a large fine will be issued.

Making the move

Since it is obvious that no-one is likely to buy a property in Italy together with its furniture nor would be advised to do so, it is necessary to decide whether to import your own furniture from the UK or buy afresh in Italy. If you are making a permanent move, you will probably prefer to bring your own things with you. In many cases, this will be a very sensible decision because many items are more expensive in Italy and (particularly with carpets or curtains) are often of lesser quality. A possible exception is if you are going to live in one of the hotter parts of Italy and none of your furniture is suitable for such a climate. On the Mediterranean coast, one can live for more than six months of the year out of doors and hot sunshine and the salt atmosphere of the sea ruins antique furniture.

Importing goods duty free

There is absolutely no need to be concerned over this problem or to consider it as part of your decision of what, or where, to buy as your new home. The rules for the import duty and tax freedom of household goods to furnish a home in Italy are simple and generous. Provided that you have owned them for at least six months and have paid VAT on them in the UK (antiques are free in any case) you may freely import all your personal belongings, furniture and furnishings for use in your new permanent home. All that is needed is an inventory (in Italian) in triplicate together with proof that you have a home in Italy. This can be in the form of a Residence Certificate (*Certificato di Residenza*) or a copy of your lease or, if you have just bought a house and cannot reside in it due to lack of furniture a letter from the Mayor (*Sindaco*) of your local municipality saying that you have come to live there. Alternatively, a copy of the *atto*, showing the purchase of your property, or a letter from the notary who dealt with the purchase which confirms you as the owner or lessee can serve. The procedure is the same whether it is for a permanent or holiday home.

You should have no trouble with the inventories. Basic Italian should suffice together with a good dictionary. Values can be intelligent guesses — Italian values of English items would be different anyway. Caution should be taken with the television set: you must be prepared to pay for at least a three month television licence **on entering the country**. This is before you know whether your set works or not! This is one of the taxes the Italian government takes seriously and they are able to collect with relative ease.

Otherwise, all electrical equipment used in the UK can be used in Italy but you must check on microwave ovens (which simply may not work if they are not the right sort for Italy), gas ovens (which must be passed by the Italian gas board) and certain electrical equipment which could have a different loading. Bear in mind the average dwelling has only three kw of electricity available so electric cookers are ruled out without a second electricity supply contract and even then they are not a good idea with the average modern cooker using something like eight or nine kw when everything is switched on.

These rules for importing your goods are based on Common Market procedures in use all over the EC so they should not vary. It is, however, as well to check them at the time you want to make use of them.

The best way to get your belongings to Italy is to use a removals firm which specialises in Italy. It is frustrating to do it yourself although it is possible provided you have unending patience and large reserves of calm. The Italian Customs can insist that you use a specialist firm known as an *Agenzia in Dogana* or an *Agenzia di Sdoganamento* and because you are doing it yourself they will charge you a fine price for a small amount of work, just to teach you a lesson.

Using a removal firm

You may be surprised at how expensive such a move can be and it is certainly desirable to get a number of estimates. References from satisfied friends or other clients are comforting. If you do not have too much furniture, try to arrange a part load so that you are sharing the cost with someone else.

Insurance

Do not forget that it is standard procedure for many removal firms to avoid liability for loss or damage to your goods in transit. On the whole, it is safer to arrange insurance yourself for a suitable amount against every possible misfortune that could overtake your goods. Too often the cover that removal firms give is only for fire and theft and there is no cover for crossing the Channel or for breakages en route. There is no problem about values, which should be realistic for insurance purposes, since whatever these may be, no duties are normally payable in Italy. If you are tempted to do your own removal, you may well have insurance problems.

16 Health and health insurance

Holiday insurance for tourists

It is a totally false economy not to take out health insurance when you go abroad. A large number of British insurance companies offer policies to cover all that you might need if you fall ill or have an accident when you are on holiday. Your travel agent will organise a policy for you or if you are making your own travel arrangements, ask your insurance broker to do what is necessary. Make certain that whatever policy you have, it covers you for repatriation to the UK if this becomes necessary. If you already have a private health policy, you will find that most of them will cover you on holiday but you must make enquiries how far this cover extends. You will probably find that it is available only for a number of weeks per year and there may be special rules if you travel out of Western Europe; check also the repatriation situation.

It is highly desirable to insure your baggage when you travel. Airlines are adept at losing baggage and stops on the motorway for lunch (no alcohol please) are often an invitation to thieves even if your car is locked. It is best, if at all possible, to take turns watching the car.

Reciprocal medical care

You can rely on the EC reciprocal medical care arrangements

alone when you go to Italy by getting a Form E 111 before you leave the UK but you would not be sensible to rely only on this. The system works well enough provided you are happy to be treated in what is a straightforward National Health hospital usually without frills. Often such a hospital will take you in and treat you without cost on the basis of a Form E 111 alone, but sometimes you are asked to pay in advance, leaving you to recover what you have paid out from Britain. In some cases, it is necessary to phone the DSS Overseas Branch in Newcastle to get a form E 112 sent out to you; this then allows you to have treatment without payment.

You can get treatment from doctors with this form E 112 but again you will almost certainly have to pay out their fee and reclaim it later. The proportion that will be refunded to you will depend on whether you have consulted a doctor wholly within the Italian NHS or one who is in the scheme but permitted to charge higher fees when not working in a hospital or state clinic, ie when you consult him at his home or surgery *(ambulatorio)*.

It is worthwhile making enquiries before you leave home about IAMAT or the International Association for Medical Assistance to Travellers, which provides English speaking doctors, in many of the large towns in Italy, who charge somewhat reduced fees. Its European Office is at 57, Voirets, Grand Lancy, Geneva, Switzerland. Local consuls will also provide the name of suitable English speaking doctors and hospitals.

You will have no difficulty in finding chemists in Italy, since it is a country which seems to have more than its fair share. In the larger towns at least, you should be able to get the medicines you are used to at home although they may come under another name. It is sensible however to take your own supply of drugs if you are on some special course of treatment. Some chemists in Italy are closed on Monday morning but there is always one chemist in every place open then and in the evenings and over weekends. It is called the *farmacia di torno* (or duty chemist).

Medical provision for residents

The Italian National Health Scheme (*Il Servizio Sanitario Nazionale*) is run by local boards known as the USL standing for *Unità Sanitaria Locale*, and is available to UK nationals who become resident in Italy in three circumstances

- You are working in Italy. In this case you will be obliged, just as anyone working in the UK is obliged, to pay National Insurance contributions to the INPS (*Instituto Nazionale di Previdenza e Salute*) and this will cover you for a pension (after a minimum of 15 years) and free treatment with the local doctor (as in the UK) and hospitalisation. The contribution you will pay will depend on your income. However, those persons who are self-employed and who do not earn almost 7.5 million lire a year will not get cover for either a pension or national health and will need to be covered by their husband or wife, father or mother or privately. They still have to pay a proportion (around 7.5%) of their gross income to the INPS. This is the most basic cover and many Italians 'top' this up by taking out private insurance or belonging to a *mutua* (see Glossary) which enables them to go to a private clinic instead of a public ward. Anywhere south of Rome Italian hospitals are pretty primitive and out of the big cities (and sometimes even in them) hospitals are no place to be ill in.

- You are living in Italy but not working. You may join the Scheme if you wish or join a *mutua*. Your contribution will be based on your income which means that you have to submit a copy of your latest Italian tax return or be assessed at the highest rate. For such doubtful returns this would be madness. You would be well advised to take out private medical insurance in the UK (see below) and rely on it alone. If you are worried about a pension then you should consult a specialist British insurance broker on this matter. In any event the premiums for both these items would be cheaper than joining a very doubtful Italian National Health Service.

- You are living in Italy and have reached retirement age. Since you will be in receipt of a UK retirement pension, you (and your wife) will be entitled to the medical benefits of the Italian NHS free of all contributions. All you need to do is to obtain from the DSS in Newcastle a form E121 and present this to your local USL and you will be registered and issued with a green card which will carry your number and the name of the local doctor with whom you are registered. Of course, if you come to Italy before you reach retirement age and keep up your DSS contributions or have sufficient contributions to give you a retirement pension, you will be sent automatically a form E121 at the right time. If you were in the Italian scheme before then, on registering as a foreign pensioner your payments to INPS will cease, unless of course you continue working in which case you will be unable to claim your pension, unless you earn under the current limit of the Italian equivalent to £75 per week.

Except as an old age pensioner you will find you end up paying something for your prescriptions (and just as in the UK there are certain drugs not available on the Italian NHS) and this is why you should also belong to a *mutua* who will pick up the bills that the state will not, will ensure you get a room to yourself (or at least with only one other person) in hospital and will get you the operation you need without your having to join a longer waiting list than exists in the UK.

Employed persons will be given the name of the *mutua* which either the company recommends or the profession which you exercise forces you to join. Some *mutua* are also insurance companies and are available to the public provided they have social security cover as well. Be very careful of joining an Italian *mutua* without having social security backing yourself. You may end up paying more than you think reasonable. In this case, if you are allowed to do so, you should opt for a British private health insurance. The same warning goes for those taking out winter sports insurance. Too often Italian schemes offer only a 'topping up' payment — they assume you already have social security which may not be the case.

Medical insurance

There are now many companies in the UK which will give you medical insurance when you are resident in Italy. Indeed, you may already have got medical cover in the UK and most companies will allow you to switch to an international scheme. On the whole, you will probably do better if you stick with the company which covered you in the UK but there are a number of very important points to consider before you decide either to stay with your existing company or to choose a new company.

- Will it restrict your travel abroad?
- Will it cover repatriation costs (presumably to the UK) in cases of major illness or death?
- What exclusions are there for illnesses you have had?
- Are there any illnesses and/or treatments not covered?
- What level of hospital costs are covered?
- Will it cover nursing at home costs?
- Will it cover other members of your family?
- Is there an age limit for joining the scheme?
- Is there an age limit for provision of benefits?
- Will the premium increase when you reach a certain age?
- Is there a qualification period before the end of which you cannot claim benefits?

Watch carefully the terms on which you can get out-patients treatment under such a policy. Many schemes now allow day-care in hospitals for serious out-patient treatment such as exploration and scanning.

Provision for death

In virtually all of Italy, cemeteries currently in use belong to local authorities and although the cost of funerals in Italy can be high, the general arrangements are much the same as in the UK. However, it often comes as a surprise that the dead must be buried within 24 hours of the event. Only if there is to be a post-mortem can this be longer.

No problems arise about funerals for people of various faiths. However, away from the large cities it is difficult to find Jewish undertakers and Jewish cemeteries partly because Italian Jews before the last war had become so assimilated and partly because there are now so few. The local British Consul should be able to help in such matters and he will also have a list of the nearest Church of England priests.

Buying a burial plot does not necessarily mean you have bought something for ever. It can be for as little as five years. Normally it is for around thirty or forty years. However, if you buy a place in a vault this is for ever and, of course, these are more expensive. Although Italy is the home of marble and granite and labour is said to be less expensive, monumental masons are very expensive and you would be wise to get a written estimate (*preventivo*) before committing yourself.

It is best to leave all the arrangements to the undertakers (known in Italian as *pompe funebri*) but try to make certain that these arrangements correspond with your wishes and not with what the undertakers think that the typical Italian family wants. Italian death certificates show the cause of death and an international death certificate will be issued where necessary. If the body is to be taken back to the UK it must undergo a special embalming process and have a special type of coffin. All undertakers know about this. It should be remembered though that returning a body to the UK for burial will cost in the region of £6,000 to £7,000 and Italy is by no means one of the more expensive countries for this service. A well-done, ordinary funeral would cost less than a sixth of that. There are no problems about cremation except that there are not many crematoria in Italy and such as there are, are near large cities. It is essential that the person who wishes to be cremated leaves **written** wishes to that effect either in the Will or by letter. Without such written instructions cremation cannot normally take place. Cremations tend to be marginally more expensive than normal burial.

You may leave your body or any organ for research but it is as well to have made arrangements prior to the death. It is a complicated process and although much to be recommended from a medical point of view is not one to be undertaken lightly in Italy.

Old age

There are now more and more specialised homes for the elderly and infirm in Italy as families, particularly in the north and in industrial areas, are no longer able to shelter both sets of in laws until they die. Most of these homes are run by the Roman Catholic Church and usually only Roman Catholics have access to them. For the non-Catholic there are occasional retirement homes run by the local municipalities but they are few and far between and there is a long waiting list. There are no specialised homes or apartments in Italy as yet, which have a warden on call or sometimes a resident nurse or doctor.

Most English people who can no longer cope with looking after themselves tend to return to the UK since they usually have not become fully integrated into the Italian way of life, a fact which becomes particularly acute when they find that life in an Italian rest home (*casa di riposo*) lacks any sort of privacy and that the health care, such as it is, is often very basic. The food too will be strange, for no matter how much one enjoys Italian food the sort of food one gets in a rest home is far from being a good advertisement for *la cucina italiana*.

One must be realistic about this sort of thing. Returning to the UK at 70 is far easier than doing so at 80 which can present your family with a major problem. By and large the price you receive for your flat or house in Italy should pay for a specialist retirement apartment or can be invested to pay part or all of the costs for a rest home.

17 Italian succession law

It is difficult to believe but there are still a lot of people who do not make their Wills. Perhaps they think that making a Will is tempting fate or perhaps they feel the formalities are complicated; often they cannot make up their mind about who to appoint as executors. In most countries, and certainly in the UK the way in which your property will be distributed if you die without leaving a Will (this is called 'dying intestate') is based on what is assumed you would have said had you made a Will but often this is far from what you wanted to happen.

As a non-Italian national you are at liberty to leave your property to whom you wish and if you do not leave any sort of Will your property will devolve according to your nationality which if you are British will be according to English or Scottish law. However, since many western European nations include the relatives of the testator irrespective of his wishes this can also act to the disadvantage of, for instance, other Europeans. If you are an Italian national you will be forced to leave your children, or if there are none, certain of your relatives, an absolute right in part of your estate.

Italian Wills

As a British subject you are also at liberty to make an Italian Will (though this is not to be generally recommended for a foreigner for many reasons, not least the language problem and the lack of knowledge about the Italian legal system) and these come in three types as described below.

Un Testamento Olografo

This must be entirely in your own handwriting and done at one sitting in the same ink — it cannot have a codicil added to it — and it has the tendency to 'disappear' at the death of the testator. On no account must it be witnessed since that will mean it will not all be in the handwriting of the testator. It is not at all to be recommended. It could be said that it would be almost better to die intestate!

Un Testamento Pubblico

This forms part of the public records of the notary with whom you lodge the document. They will prepare it for you, charge you a fee as would your solicitor and file it away. Thus, there is no chance of loss or forgery. It is witnessed in the notary's office. This is by far the best type of Will to make if you are an Italian national or if you are a foreigner who insists upon an Italian Will.

Un Testamento Segreto

This is another type of Will which is not highly recommended since it is a mixture of the preceding two. The testator writes the Will and hands it to the notary for safe keeping. This last and the first type of Will are of the 'home-made' type which are usually so badly expressed that they often require expensive 'interpretation'. Incidentally, it is a requirement of Italian law that everyone, including foreigners making an Italian Will, must state their nationality, place and date of birth.

Since everyone is going to die at sometime, the most economical way of arranging your affairs is to have an English or Scottish lawyer prepare a Will for you. On no account put it in a strongbox in an Italian bank since the Will has to be proved before access can be gained to the strongbox! If all your assets are in Italy you will almost certainly find that you will have a safe for insurance purposes and this is the best place to keep it. Alternatively, if your house in Italy is for holidays then your Will will cover assets in the UK as well and your solicitor can safeguard it for you.

Your solicitor in the UK should be aware of how property owned by foreigners in Italy devolves — if he appears not to know you should inform him.

At your death your Will is proved in the UK in the normal way. It then goes for translation via the Italian Consulate who will stamp it and either return it to the solicitor or Italian notary involved. Thereafter, the assets are transferred.

Wills made in the Italian form, ie Italian Wills, do not go back to the country of the testator to be proved but are proved in Italy.

Two Wills

Occasionally, for those who are **resident** in Italy but who have property elsewhere it can be to the advantage of the surviving spouse that two Wills are made, one English (or Scottish) and one Italian. This leads you into the domain of the international lawyer but it can mean that you are able to avoid paying Italian inheritance tax on property in England left to a surviving spouse, where, in that country, no duty is payable. It is, of course, essential that the two Wills do not overlap and that the Italian Will deals only with property **situate** in Italy, ie the family house, Italian shares, etc. The English Will will deal with the rest of the estate.

For those with holiday homes only and who are **not** resident in Italy there is no point in making an Italian Will since it achieves nothing and you will not be charged inheritance tax on your spouse's assets in the UK. You will, however, pay duty on property in Italy owned by your husband or wife.

Inheritance tax

So far the testator has had it all his own way. If you are resident in the UK then UK inheritance tax is due on all assets above £118,000 unless these are left to a spouse. If there is property in Italy **it is the beneficiary who pays the inheritance tax** and on a scale according to the relationship with the testator. Thus children and parents pay less than the spouse and the rate increases as the relationship becomes remoter. There is absolutely no relief for a surviving spouse in Italy although a life interest for a surviving spouse can be given and this is the best way to avoid paying too much inheritance tax or paying twice. This means that the children who inherit the property cannot dispossess the widow or widower during her or his lifetime and indeed should, in the event of the life tenant wishing to move, purchase a similar property. For all practical purposes, until the children are all 18, selling the property is impossible since a *tutore* or guardian will have been appointed by the Italian court — even though the surviving spouse may own the other half of the property. From a tax point of view, however, inheritance tax will be payable as between the dead parent and the children. The life interest to the surviving spouse carries no tax.

Rates

Compared with many countries Italian inheritance tax is not onerous particularly where it is the children who inherit. All estates worth under 30 million lire are exempt from duty and the highest rate of duty is around 30% payable on an estate worth in excess of 1,000 million (about £450,000). But when a totally unrelated person inherits he starts paying tax after the first million lire at three per cent and pays 60% on amounts above 1,000 million lire. Thus if someone leaves her dearest friend a diamond brooch, valued at probate at 2,000,000 lire the friend will pay 30,000 lire to the government to obtain it whereas had she left it to her daughter she would have paid nothing, assuming there was not a great deal of other property involved.

Valuation

The valuation of property is usually done by the valuer of the local *comune* or by a specialist appointed by them. As in most countries the probate valuation is a little lower than the market value, particularly if there is a life interest for a surviving spouse, but it is difficult to question what you may consider too high a valuation.

An annual tax is chargeable on all property and land and this is payable to the *comune* where the property is situate. A lot of foreigners do not know about this tax (those who make an annual income tax return will) and years go by without it being paid. This can mount up since there is not only the amount to pay but an annual fine for not paying it. All this annual tax (ILOR) plus the fines must be paid before the property can be transferred. There are a vast number of British who revel in the fact that there are no real 'rates' to pay in Italy, except for water and rubbish disposal. They are very often sitting on an expensive time bomb. Over a period of, say, twelve years this tax and its accompanying fines for non-payment could come to some three or four million lire when the tax itself was only 100,000 lire a year!

Settling the estate

Because these taxes and inheritance tax have to be paid before the property is transferred to the beneficiary, finding the money can become a problem. It is, of course, possible to take out an endowment policy (not subject to inheritance tax) to cover this eventuality and it is also possible to borrow from a UK or Italian bank — though the former are cheaper — until such time as the other assets in the estate are realised. Failure to pay the taxes within two years of death incurs interest.

Settling an estate takes time in Italy and those who do not goad the notary almost weekly get put to the bottom of the pile — that is a fact of life in most notarial offices. Therefore, you should avail yourself of the services of an Italian *avvocato* who will intervene for you and see that things are done. You should not, however, expect miracles.

Unlike many countries the Italians are not very interested in what you inherit out of Italy and will not seek to tax you on what you inherit from your mother, uncle or friend in Britain. Of course, if you are an Italian resident and inherit from your husband or wife under a Will which mentions both property in the UK and Italy which you owned jointly, then you will need to consult an *avvocato* (**not** a notary at this stage) who will sort things out for you. What decision you make about your Will or Wills depends on how this chapter affects you. If you recall nothing but the need to seek legal advice of the right kind then it was worth reading. The Law Society will give names of lawyers who specialise in Italian law. The other important thing is that you must keep your Will up to date as your circumstances change. An out of date Will can be as unsatisfactory as no Will at all, although even that may prove more beneficial than a 'home-made' attempt.

Endnote

In spite of the constant warnings in this book of what can go wrong you will probably find that living in Italy, particularly in the countryside, is not at all problematical or difficult. This is provided that when in doubt you ask the relevant authority whether or not you can do something rather than just acting and pleading ignorance later on and also provided you do not assume that things are the same in Italy as in the UK. They are not and that is part of the reason you have chosen to buy property in Italy — to say nothing of the price!

By and large the Italians are kind, helpful, make good neighbours and have a marvellous capacity for enjoying life to the full. Of course there are always exceptions as in every country but somehow they seem rarer in Italy. Merely the way they happily accept foreigners says a lot for their tolerance level. Although passionately interested in politics and religion they are not bigots and will not try to convert you to their way of thinking.

If you choose Italy for its reliable climate, beautiful scenery, splendid art treasures and rather good food and drink, you will get a pleasant surprise and find that the people are the best part of the country.

As Yve Menzies says in 'Living in Italy', 'Italians should be recognised as the most human of human beings — the ideal type, if you like — and be much respected for being so. An ideal people, living in what is, in every way, an ideal land.'

Appendix

The diagram on pages 132–133 is an example of an Italian electricity bill. The numbers on the illustration correspond to the points listed below.

ENEL — your bill in detail

1 Office issuing bill.
2 Consumer's name and address.
3 Consumer's number.
4 Date covered by this bill.
5 ENEL's code as to zone and payment.
6 Type of electricity supply — domestic and amount — 3 kw.
7 Reckoning up for previous six month period January-June together with last reading, present reading and total consumption.
8 Total cost in lire of consumption.
9 Deduction of amounts already paid on estimated bills.
10 Amount owed as a result of reckoning up.
11 Standing charge for 3 kw supply.
12 Brought forward from Item 10.
13 Total amount subject to VAT (IVA).
14 Last day for payment.
15 Total VAT (IVA) imposed.
16 Amount taken as deposit on connecting the supply. (Returnable.)
17 Rounding up or down from previous and present bill to make even sum.
18 Total sum payable.
19 The whole of this section is blanked out because it will be paid by direct debit from consumer's bank account.

1 2

TASSA PAGATA · TARIFFA FATTURA
AUTORIZZAZIONE DCCP/1/1/1853
ST/72/Lo del 30 OTTOBRE 1972

ENEL COMPARTIMENTO DI TORINO

ZONA DI IMPERIA
PZA DELLA VITTORIA 3
18100 IMPERIA
TEL. 0183/ 274406

FATTURA COMMERCIALE

MARTINI, ANNA
via PALAZZO 22

18032 BORDIGHERA (IM)

12 1

C. C. P. PREMARCATO

Ricevuta di un versamento o certificato di addebito *sul c/c n.* 30 6122 *intestato a:* CODICE FISCALE E PARTITA IVA — Vedere retro

COD CA	DESCRIZIONE	IMPORTI (LIRE)
20	PERIODO LUG 89-AGO 89 - QUOTA FISSA	860
16	ACCONTO N. 1 SUL CONSUMO (KWH 616)	8257
	DI CUI L 2526 IMPOSTA ERAR E L 8388 ENTI LOCALI	
	N.B. DAL 1.1.89 PARTITA IVA ENEL 00934061003	
	ADDEBITATA S.B.F. SU C/C CREDIT	

SCADENZA (1)	IMPONIBILE IVA	%	IMPORTO IVA	NON ASSOGGETTATO AD IVA	GIA ASSOGGETTATO AD IVA	ARR PREC	ARR ATT	TOTALE LIRE
23/ 8/89	91172	9	8206			48	-26	******994

NUMERO UTENTE U FATT
0867402602048 1 4

PERIODO: LUG-AGO 89

ZONA	EM	GR	U	ENTE PAG
4-35	36	26	0	2008000

0208

MARTINI, ANNA
via PALAZZO 22
18032 BORDIGHERA (IM) SCALA PIANO INT

SPAZIO RISERVATO AI CORRENTISTI POSTALI
Titolare del c/c n

ADDI
Bollo a data
tassa
Bollo lineare dell'ufficio accettante
l'Ufficiale postale
data progress.
Certificato del bollettino

30000
ANTICIPO SUL CONSUMO (3)

INDIRIZZO DELLA FORNITURA SE DIVERSO DAL RECAPITO DI ESAZIONE

P140 195522
(1)-(2)-(3)-(4) Vedere avvertenze a tergo

14 16 13 15 17 18

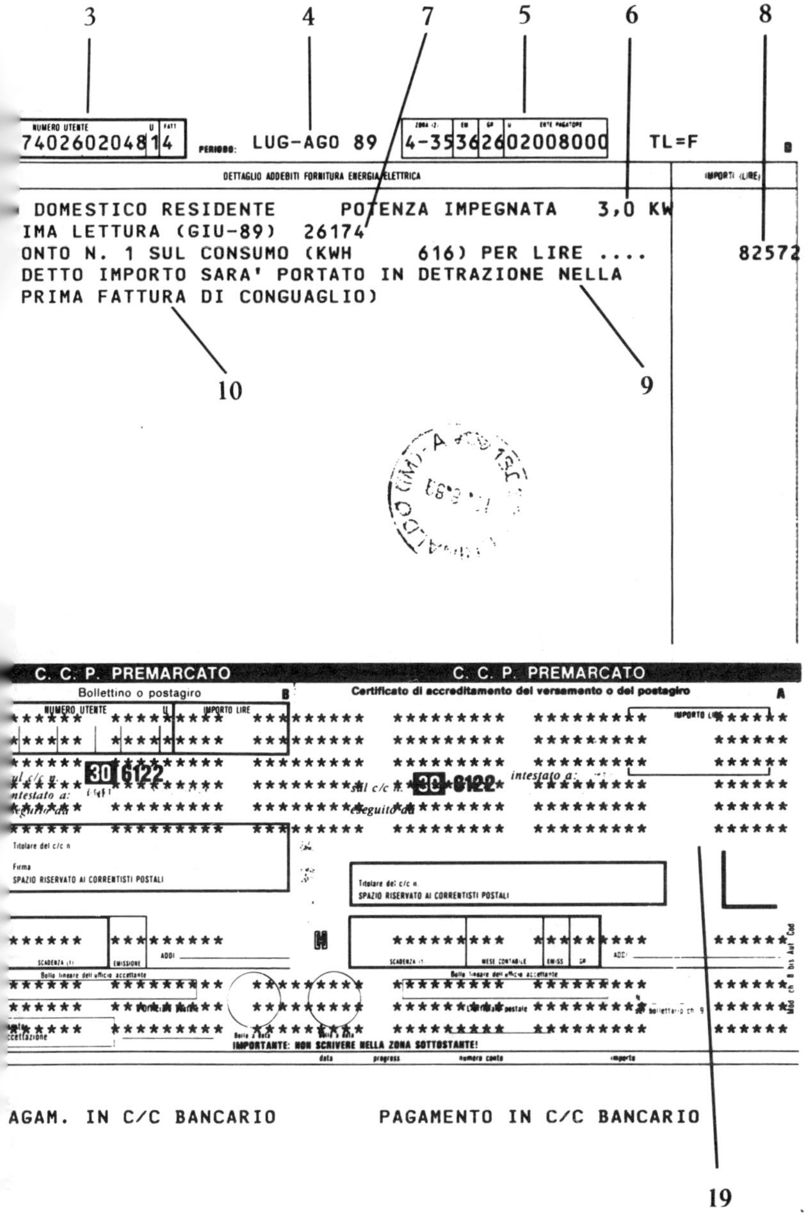
3
4
7
5
6
8
NUMERO UTENTE
7402602048 1 4
PERIODO: LUG-AGO 89
4-353 6 2602008000
TL=F
DETTAGLIO ADDEBITI FORNITURA ENERGIA ELETTRICA
IMPORTI (LIRE)
DOMESTICO RESIDENTE POTENZA IMPEGNATA 3,0 KW
IMA LETTURA (GIU-89) 26174
ONTO N. 1 SUL CONSUMO (KWH 616) PER LIRE ....
82572
DETTO IMPORTO SARA' PORTATO IN DETRAZIONE NELLA
PRIMA FATTURA DI CONGUAGLIO)
10
9
C. C. P. PREMARCATO
C. C. P. PREMARCATO
Bollettino o postagiro
Certificato di accreditamento del versamento o del postagiro
NUMERO UTENTE
IMPORTO LIRE
30 6122
intestato a:
eseguito da
Titolare del c/c n.
Firma
SPAZIO RISERVATO AI CORRENTISTI POSTALI
SCADENZA
EMISSIONE
MESE CONTABILE
Bollo lineare dell'ufficio accettante
IMPORTANTE: NON SCRIVERE NELLA ZONA SOTTOSTANTE!
data
progress
numero conto
importo
AGAM. IN C/C BANCARIO
PAGAMENTO IN C/C BANCARIO
19

Glossary

Agenzia in dogana — Customs clearing agent.
Agenzia di sdoganamento — Customs clearing agent.
Ambulatorio — a doctor's or a vet's surgery visited by the public.
Administratore — the administrator, usually of a company or a block of flats known as a *condominio*.
Assegno — cheque.
Assegno circolare — bank draft.
Assegno a vuoto — cheque issued without funds to cover it.
Atto — a legal act or transfer, such as transfer of property.
Autorità di Procura — Power of Attorney.
Avvocato — a lawyer.
Azienda Agricola — an agricultural company or organisation.

Bolletta — account such as telephone bill — *bolletta* SIP, or electricity — *bolletta luce o ENEL.*
Bollo — stamp for documents, also receipt for road fund tax. *Marca di bollo* — stamps put on driving licence each year.
Bombole — gas bottle.
Bombolone — gas tank, usually 900 or 1500 litres.

Camera di Commercio — Chamber of Commerce.
Carabinieri — the military police force under the Ministry of Defence who do much of the policing of country districts.
Carta bollata — Revenue stamped paper — most documents in Italy require the use of this paper.
Cassa — till (at bank or in an office, shop etc).
Cassa di Risparmio di . . . — Savings Bank of (name of province or area).

Certificato di Residenza — Residence Certificate.
Collaudo — an examination, followed by a report, on cars, boats, houses etc.
Commercialistà — a qualified accountant.
Commissione Edilizia — Building (Planning) Committee.
Compromesso — contract for the sale and purchaser of land.
Comune — local authority (the smallest entity) — other places are described as *Città di, Provincia di, Regione di* (the largest entity).
Condominio — a block of flats or a large private house owned by a number of people.
Condono edilizio — a method, only sometimes allowed, of paying a fine for building work which has been done without planning permission. There is always a scale fine to pay, sometimes very large. A dangerous method to adopt.
Confino — edge or frontier of a country, as in *Confino di Stato*. Also, under the Fascists, a lonely and usually inhospitable area in which to place enemies of the State so they were out of contact with the rest of Italy and the world at large.
Conguaglio — a reckoning up statement. Usually done by ENEL or the Gas company every six months.
Consiglio — a council, usually of a block of flats or local authority.
Contratto d'Affito — a lease.

Dichiarazione di Soggiorno per Stranieri — Foreigners' Declaration of Stay in Italy. Made at the local town hall in the first instance then at the State Police or *Carabinieri*.
Differenziale — earth trip (electricity).
Dogana — Italian Customs and Excise. The word comes from the Doges of Venice who were the first to impose such charges on entry of goods or transhipments through Venice.

ENEL — The Italian national electricity board. Letters stand for *Ente Nazionale per l'Energia Elettrica*.

Ente condominiale — the condominium and all that pertains to it.
Equo canone — fair rent charges, as set out in the Italian rent acts from time to time.
Estratto di Conto corrente — Bank Statement (Current Account).
Farmacia di torno — duty chemist, ie who is bound to be open when others are shut.
Fondazione — state recognised charity.

Geometrà — surveyor, architect and administrator combined.
Gettone — telephone token, currently 200 lire each.
Guardia di Finanza — Financial Police, Customs and Fraud Squad all rolled into one.

ILOR — *Imposte locale sui Reditti.* A local tax charged on income but which is deductible from the normal income tax paid.
Imposte di — *donazione* — gift tax,
successione — inheritance tax,
INPS — *Istituto Nazionale di Previdenza e Salute.* The Italian National Insurance Scheme and National Health Service.
INVIM — Italian capital gains tax.
IRPEF — *Imposte sui Reditti di Persone Fisiche* — Personal income tax.
IVA — *Imposte sul Valore Aggiunto* ie Italian VAT.

Libretto d'assegni — cheque book.
Licenza — permission or licence, to build etc.

Municipio — local authority's office, town hall.
Mutua — a form of insurance which 'tops up' Italian Social Security services; joining a *mutua* will enable you to have your own room in hospital, see specialists quickly, etc.

Notaio or *notaro* — a notary. The Italian State Official who transfers property and land from one person to another and then registers the transaction and pays over the stamp duties etc to the State.

Numero di Codice Fiscale — Fiscal Code number — everyone owning property in Italy has one. Used mostly for VAT (IVA) purposes.
Polizia di Stats — State Police.
Pompe funebri — funeral directors.
Preventivo — estimate (for work etc to be undertaken).
Procura — see *Autorità di Procura.*
Progetto — project or design for obtaining planning consent.
Promessi di Vendità — unilateral offer to sell (usually land or houses), usually valid for a short period and binding on the seller when accepted by a purchaser.

Regolomento del Condominio — Condominium management, rules, regulations and charges.

Salva vita — earth trip.
Separazione dei beni — type of marriage contract in Italy where each party to a marriage owns his/her own property and not in community of property.
Servitù di passagio — *d'acqua* etc, ie right of way or easement.
Servitù di necessità — a right of way that must be given to landlocked property.
Sindaco — mayor (usually of small city or of a *comune*).
SIP — *Società Italiana per l'Esercizio delle Telecomunicazioni p.a.*

Tagliando — stub or receipt, such as you receive for a Giro payment.
Testamento — Will.

Unità Immobiliare — proportion of common parts of block owned by any flat in that block and on which service charges are based.
USL — *Unità Sanitaria Locale* — the local office of the Italian National Health Service.

Vasca — small water reservoir found all over the countryside in Italy.

Index

Other titles in this series

Managing Your Finances	Helen Pridham
Planning Your Pension	Tony Reardon
Buying Your Home	Richard Newell
Running Your Own Business	David Williams
Tax for the Self-Employed	David Williams
Your Home in Portugal	Rosemary de Rougemont
Your Home in Spain	Per Svensson
Planning School and College Fees	Danby Bloch & Amanda Pardoe
Investing in Shares	Hugh Pym & Nick Kochan
Insurance: Are You Covered?	Mihir Bose
Leaving Your Money Wisely	Tony Foreman
Financial Planning for the Over 50s	Robert Leach
Your Home in France	Henry Dyson
Making your Job Work	David Williams
Tax and Finance for Women	Helen Pridham